Another Day of Life

RYSZARD KAPUŚCIŃSKI

Another Day of Life

TRANSLATED FROM THE POLISH BY
WILLIAM R. BRAND AND
KATARZYNA MROCZKOWSKA-BRAND

A Helen and Kurt Wolff Book
Harcourt Brace Jovanovich, Publishers
San Diego   New York   London

HBJ

Originally published in Polish under the title
Jeszcze dzień życia

Library of Congress Cataloging-in-Publication Data

Kapuściński, Ryszard.
    Another day of life.

    Translation of: Jeszcze dzień życia.
    "A Helen and Kurt Wolff book."
    1. Kapuściński, Ryszard.
2. Angola—History—Revolution, 1961–1975—Personal
narratives.   3. Angola—History—Revolution, 1961–
1975—Journalists.   4. Journalists—Poland—Biography.
I. Title.
DT611.76.K37A313   1986   967′.303   86-10002
ISBN 0-15-107563-8

Designed by Kaelin Chappell

Printed in the United States of America

First edition

A   B   C   D   E

O, Lord!

Despite a great many prayers to You we are continually losing our wars. Tomorrow we shall again be fighting a battle that is truly great. With all our might we need Your help and that is why I must tell You something: This battle tomorrow is going to be a serious affair. There will be no place in it for children. Therefore I must ask You not to send Your Son to help us. Come Yourself.

—the prayer of Koq, leader of the Griquas tribe, before a battle with the Afrikaners in 1876

Abbreviations

FNLA   National Front for the Liberation of Angola, led by Holden Roberto and backed by the Western powers and Zaïre

MPLA   Popular Movement for the Liberation of Angola, led by Agostinho Neto and backed by the Soviet Union and Cuba

UNITA   National Union for the Total Independence of Angola, led by Jonas Savimbi and backed by the Western powers and South Africa

PIDE   Portuguese political police

PAP   Polish Press Agency

This is a very personal book, about being alone and lost. In summer 1975 my boss—at the time I was a correspondent for a press agency—said, "This is your last chance to get to Angola. How about it?" I always answer yes in such situations. (The reason he asked me the way he did was that the civil war which continues to this day was already under way. Many were convinced that the country would turn into a hell—and a closed hell at that, in which everyone would die without any outside help or intervention.) The war had begun in the spring of that year, when the new rulers of Portugal, after the overthrow of the Salazar dictatorship, gave Angola and Portugal's other former colonies the right to independence. In Angola there were several political parties—armed to the teeth—doing battle with one another, and each of these parties wanted to take power at any price (most often, at the price of their brothers' blood).

The war these parties waged among themselves was sloppy,

dogged, and cruel. *Everyone was everyone's enemy, and no one was sure who would meet death. At whose hands, when, and where. And why. All those who could were fleeing Angola. I was bent on going there. In Lisbon I convinced the crew of one of the last Portuguese military aircraft flying to Angola to take me along. More precisely, I begged them to take me.*

The next morning I saw from the window of our descending plane a motionless white patch surrounded by the sun. It was Luanda.

Part I

Part I

For three months I lived in Luanda, in the Tivoli Hotel. From my window I had a view of the bay and the port. Offshore stood several freighters under European flags. Their captains maintained radio contact with Europe and they had a better idea of what was happening in Angola than we did—we were imprisoned in a besieged city. When the news circulated around the world that the battle for Luanda was approaching, the ships sailed out to sea and stopped on the edge of the horizon. The last hope of rescue receded with them, since escape by land was impossible, and rumors said that at any moment the enemy would bombard and immobilize the airport. Later it turned out that the date for the attack on Luanda had been changed and the fleet returned to the bay, expecting as always to load cargoes of cotton and coffee.

The movement of these ships was an important source of information for me. When the bay emptied, I began preparing for the worst. I listened, trying to hear if the sound of artillery barrages was approaching. I wondered if there was any truth in what the Portuguese whispered among themselves, that two thousand of Holden Roberto's soldiers were hiding in the city, waiting only for orders to begin the slaughter. But in the middle of these anxieties the ships sailed back into the bay. In my mind I hailed the sailors I had never met as saviors: it would be quiet for a while.

In the next room lived two old people: Don Silva, a diamond merchant, and his wife Dona Esmeralda, who was dying of cancer. She was passing her last days without help or comfort, since the hospitals were closed and the doctors had left. Her body, twisted in pain, was disappearing among a heap of pillows. I was afraid to go into the room. Once I entered to ask if it bothered her when I typed at night. Her thoughts broke free of the pain for a moment, long enough for her to say, "No, Ricardo, I haven't got enough time left to be bothered by anything."

Don Silva paced the corridors for hours. He argued with everyone, cursed the world, carried a chip on his shoulder. He even yelled at blacks, though by this time everybody was treating them politely and one of our neighbors had even got into the habit of stopping Africans he didn't know from Adam, shaking hands, and bowing low. They thought the war had got to him and hurried away. Don Silva was waiting for the arrival of Holden Roberto and kept asking me if I knew anything on that score. The sight of the ships sailing away filled him with the keenest joy. He rubbed his hands, straightened up, and showed his false teeth.

Despite the overwhelming heat, Don Silva always dressed in warm clothes. He had strings of diamonds sewn into the pleats of his suit. Once, in a flush of good humor when it seemed that the FNLA was already at the entrance to the hotel, he showed me a handful of transparent stones that looked like fragments of crushed glass. They were diamonds. Around the hotel it was said that Don Silva carried half a million dollars on his person. The old man's heart was torn. He wanted to escape with his riches, but Dona Esmeralda's illness tied him down. He was afraid that if he didn't leave immediately someone would report him, and his treasure would be taken away. He never went out in the street. He even wanted to install extra locks, but all the locksmiths had left and there wasn't a soul in Luanda who could do the job.

Across from me lived a young couple, Arturo and Maria. He was a colonial official and she was a silent blonde, calm, with misty, carnal eyes. They were waiting to leave, but first they had to exchange their Angolan money for Portuguese, and that took weeks because the lines at the banks stretched endlessly. Our cleaning lady, a warm, alert old woman named Dona Cartagina, reported to me in outraged whispers that Arturo and Maria were living in sin. That meant living like blacks, like those atheists from the MPLA. In her scale of values this was the lowest state of degradation and infamy a white person could reach.

Dona Cartagina was also anticipating Holden Roberto's arrival. She didn't know where his army was and would ask me secretly for news. She also asked if I was writing good things about the FNLA. I told her I was, enthusiastically. In gratitude she always cleaned my room until it shined, and when there was nothing in town to drink she brought me—from where, I don't know—a bottle of mineral water.

Maria treated me like a man who was preparing for suicide after I told her that I'd be staying in Luanda until November 11, when Angola was to become independent. In her opinion there wouldn't be a stone left standing in the city by then. Everyone would die and Luanda would turn into a great burial place inhabited by vultures and hyenas. She urged me to leave quickly. I bet her a bottle of wine that I'd survive and we'd meet in Lisbon, in the elegant Altis Hotel, at five o'clock in the afternoon of November 15. I was late for the rendezvous, but the desk clerk had a note from Maria telling me she had waited, but was leaving for Brazil with Arturo the next day.

The whole Tivoli Hotel was packed to the transoms and resembled our train stations right after the war: jammed with people by turns excited and apathetic, with stacks of shabby bundles tied together with string. It smelled bad everywhere, sour, and a sticky, choking sultriness filled the building. People were sweating from heat and from fear. There was an apocalyptic mood, an expectation of destruction. Somebody brought word that they were going to bomb the city in the night. Somebody else had learned that in their quarters the blacks were sharpening knives and wanted to try them on Portuguese throats. The uprising was to explode at any moment. What uprising? I asked, so I could write it up for Warsaw. Nobody knew exactly. Just an uprising, and we'll find out what kind of uprising when it hits us.

Rumor exhausted everyone, plucked at nerves, took away the capacity to think. The city lived in an atmosphere of hysteria and trembled with dread. People didn't know how to cope with the reality that surrounded them, how to interpret it, get used to it. Men gathered in the hotel corridors to hold councils of war. Uninspired pragmatists favored barricading the Tivoli at night. Those with wider horizons and the ability to see things in a global perspective contended that a telegram appealing for intervention ought to be sent to the UN. But, as is the Latin custom, everything ended in argument.

Every evening a plane flew over the city and dropped leaflets. The plane was painted black, with no lights or markings. The leaflets said that Holden Roberto's army was outside Luanda and would enter the capital soon, perhaps the next day. To facilitate the conquest, the populace was urged to kill all the Russians, Hungarians, and Poles who commanded the MPLA units and were the cause of the whole war and all the misfortunes that had befallen the distressed nation. This happened in September, when in all Angola there was one person from Eastern Europe—me. Gangs from PIDE were prowling the city; they would come to the hotel and ask who was staying there. They acted with impunity—no authorities existed in Luanda—and they wanted to get even for everything, for the revolution in Portugal, for the loss of Angola, for their shattered careers. Every knock at the door could mean the end for me. I tried not to think about it, which is the only thing to do in such a situation.

The PIDE gangs met in the Adao nightclub next to the hotel. It was always dark there; the waiters carried lanterns. The owner of the club, a fat, ruined playboy with swollen lids veiling his bloodshot eyes, took me into his office once. There were shelves built into the walls from floor to ceiling, and on them stood 226 brands of whisky. He took two pistols from his desk drawer and laid them down in front of him.

"I'm going to kill ten communists with these," he said, "and then I'll be happy."

I looked at him, smiled, and waited to see what he would do. Through the door I could hear music and the thugs having a good time with drunken mulatto girls. The fat man put the pistols back in the drawer and slammed it shut. To this day I don't know why he let me go. He might have been one of those people you meet sometimes who get less of a kick from killing than from knowing that they could have killed but didn't.

All September I went to bed uncertain about what would happen that night and the following day. Several types whose faces I came to know hung about. We kept running into each other but never exchanged a word. I didn't know what to do. I decided right off to stay awake—I didn't want them catching me in my sleep. But in the middle of the night the tension would ease and I'd fall asleep in my clothes, in my shoes, on the big bed that Dona Cartagina had made with such care.

The MPLA couldn't protect me. They were far away in the African quarters, or even farther away at the front. The European quarter in which I was living was not yet theirs. That's why I liked going to the front—it was safer there, more familiar. I could make such journeys only rarely, however. Nobody, not even the people from the staff, could define exactly where the front was. There was neither transport nor communications. Solitary little outfits of greenhorn partisans were lost in enormous, treacherous spaces. They moved here and there without plan or thought. Everybody was fighting a private war, everybody was on his own.

Each evening at nine, Warsaw called. The lights of

the telex machine at the hotel reception desk came on
and the printer typed out the signal:

814251 PAP PL GOOD EVENING PLEASE SEND

or:

WE FINALLY GOT THROUGH

or:

ANYTHING FOR US TODAY? PLS GA GA

I answered:

OK OK MOM SVP

and turned on the tape with the text of the dispatch.

For me, nine o'clock was the high point of the day—
a big event repeated each evening. I wrote daily. I wrote
out of the most egocentric of motives: I overcame my
inertia and depression in order to produce even the
briefest dispatch and so maintain contact with Warsaw,
because it rescued me from loneliness and the feeling of
abandonment. If there was time, I settled down at the
telex long before nine. When the light came on I felt like
a wanderer in the desert who catches sight of a spring.
I tried every trick I could think of to drag out the length
of those séances. I described the details of every battle.
I asked what the weather was like at home and complained that I had nothing to eat. But in the end came
the moment when Warsaw signed off:

GOOD RECEPTION CONTACT TOMORROW 20 HRS GMT TKS
BY BY

and the light went out and I was left alone again.

Luanda was not dying the way our Polish cities died

in the last war. There were no air raids, there was no "pacification," no destruction of district after district. There were no cemeteries in the streets and squares. I don't remember a single fire. The city was dying the way an oasis dies when the well runs dry: it became empty, fell into inanition, passed into oblivion. But that agony would come later; for the moment there was feverish movement everywhere. Everybody was in a hurry, everybody was clearing out. Everyone was trying to catch the next plane to Europe, to America, to anywhere. Portuguese from all over Angola converged on Luanda. Caravans of automobiles loaded down with people and baggage arrived from the most distant corners of the country. The men were unshaven, the woman tousled and rumpled, the children dirty and sleepy. On the way the refugees linked up in long columns and crossed the country that way, since the bigger the group, the safer it was. At first they checked into the Luanda hotels but later, when there were no vacancies, they drove straight to the airport. A nomad city without streets or houses sprang up around the airport. People lived in the open, perpetually soaked because it was always raining. They were living worse now than the blacks in the African quarter that abutted the airport, but they took it apathetically, with dismal resignation, not knowing whom to curse for their fate. Salazar was dead, Caetano had escaped to Brazil, and the government in Lisbon kept changing. The revolution was to blame for everything, they said, because before that it had been peaceful. Now the government had promised the blacks freedom and the blacks had come to blows among themselves, burning and murdering. They aren't capable of governing. Let me tell you what a black is like, they would say:

he gets drunk and sleeps all day. If he can hang some beads on himself he walks around happy. Work? Nobody works here. They live like a hundred years ago. A hundred? A thousand! I've seen ones like that, living like a thousand years ago. You ask me who knows what it was like a thousand years ago? Oh, you can tell for sure. Everybody knows what it was like. This country won't last long. Mobutu will take a hunk of it, the ones to the south will take their cut, and that's the end of it. If only I could get out this minute. And never lay eyes on it again. I put in forty years of work here. The sweat of my damn brow. Who will give it back to me now? Do you think anybody can start life all over again?

People are sitting on bundles covered with plastic because it's drizzling. They are meditating, pondering everything. In this abandoned crowd that has been vegetating here for weeks, the spark of revolt sometimes flashes. Women beat up the soldiers designated to maintain order, and men try to hijack a plane to let the world know what despair they've been driven to. Nobody knows when they will fly out or in what direction. A cosmic mess prevails. Organization comes hard to the Portuguese, avowed individualists who by nature cannot live in narrow bounds, in community. Pregnant women have priority. Why them? Am I worse because I gave birth six months ago? All right, pregnant women and those with infants have priority. Why them? Am I worse because my son just turned three? Okay, women with children have priority. Huh? And me? Just because I'm a man, am I to be left here to die? So the strongest board the plane and the women with children throw themselves on the tarmac, under the wheels, so the pilot can't taxi. The army arrives, throws the men off, orders the women aboard, and the women walk up the steps in triumph, like a victorious unit entering a newly conquered city.

Let's say we fly out the ones whose nerves have been shattered. Beautiful, look no further, because if it hadn't been for the war, I'd have been in the lunatic asylum long ago. And us in Carmona, we were raided by a band of wild men who took everything, beat us, wanted to shoot us. I've been nothing but shakes ever since. I'll go nuts if I don't fly out of here at once. My dear fellow, I'll say no more than this: I've lost the fruits of a life's work. Besides, where we lived in Lumbala two UNITA soldiers grabbed me by the hair and a third poked a gun barrel right in my eye. I consider that sufficient reason to take leave of my senses.

No criterion won general approbation. The despondent crowd swarmed around each plane, and hours passed before they could work out who finally got a seat. They have to carry half a million refugees across an air bridge to the other side of the world.

Everybody knows why they want to leave. They know they'll survive September, but October will be very bad and nobody will live through November. How do they know? How can you ask such a question? says one. I've lived here for twenty-eight years and I can tell you something about this country. Do you know what I had to show for it in the end? An old taxi that I left sitting in the street.

Do you believe it? I ask Arturo. Arturo doesn't believe it, but he still wants to leave. And you, Dona Cartagina, do you believe it? Yes, Dona Cartagina is convinced. If we stay till November, that'll be the end of us. The old lady energetically draws a finger across her throat, on which her fingernail leaves a red mark.

People escaped as if from an infectious disease, as if from pestilential air that can't be seen but still inflicts death. Afterward the wind blows and the sand drifts over the traces of the last survivor.

Various things happened before that, before the city was closed and sentenced to death. As a sick person suddenly revives and recovers his strength for a moment in the midst of his agony, so, at the end of September, life in Luanda took on a certain vigor and tempo. The sidewalks were crowded and traffic jams clogged the streets. People ran around nervously, in a hurry, wrapping up thousands of matters. Clear out as quickly as possible, escape in time, before the first wave of deadly air intrudes upon the city.

They didn't want Angola. They had had enough of the country, which was supposed to be the promised land but had brought them disenchantment and abasement. They said farewell to their African homes with mixed despair and rage, sorrow and impotence, with the feeling of leaving forever. All they wanted was to get out with their lives and to take their possessions with them.

Everybody was busy building crates. Mountains of boards and plywood were brought in. The price of hammers and nails soared. Crates were the main topic of conversation—how to build them, what was the best thing to reinforce them with. Self-proclaimed experts, crate specialists, homegrown architects of cratery, masters of crate styles, crate schools, and crate fashions appeared. Inside the Luanda of concrete and bricks a new wooden city began to rise. The streets I walked through resembled a great building site. I stumbled over discarded planks; nails sticking out of beams ripped my shirt. Some crates were as big as vacation cottages, because a hierarchy of crate status had suddenly come into being. The richer the people, the bigger the crates they erected. Crates belonging to millionaires were impressive: beamed and lined with sailcloth, they had solid, elegant walls made of the most expensive grades of tropical wood, with the rings and knots cut and polished like antiques. Into these crates went whole salons and bedrooms, sofas, tables, wardrobes, kitchens and refrigerators, commodes and armchairs, pictures, carpets, chandeliers, porcelain, bedclothes and linen, clothing, tapestries and vases, even artificial flowers (I saw them with my own eyes), all the monstrous and inexhaustible junk that clutters every middle-class home. Into them went figurines, seashells, glass balls, flower bowls, stuffed lizards, a metal miniature of the cathedral of Milan brought back from Italy, letters!—letters and photographs, wedding pictures in gilt frames (Why don't we leave that? the husband asks, and the enraged wife cries, You ought to be ashamed!)—all the pictures of the children, and here's the first time he sat up, and here's the first time he said Give, Give, and here he is with a lollipop, and here with his grandma—everything, and I mean everything, because this case of wine, this supply of macaroni that I laid in as soon as the shooting started, and then the fishing rod, the crochet needles—my yarn!—my rifle, Tutu's colored blocks, birds, peanuts, the vacuum and the nutcracker, have to be squeezed in, too, that's all there is to it, they have to be, and they are, so that all we leave behind are the bare floors, the naked walls, *en déshabille*. The house's strip-tease goes all the way, right down to the curtain rods—and all that remains is to lock the door and stop along the boulevard en route to the airport and throw the key in the ocean.

The crates of the poor are inferior on several counts. They are smaller, often downright diminutive, and unsightly. They can't compete in quality; their workmanship leaves a great deal to be desired. While the wealthy can employ master cabinetmakers, the poor have to knock their crates together with their own hands. For materials they use odds and ends from the lumber yard, mill ends, warped beams, cracked plywood, all the leftovers you can pick up thirdhand. Many are made of hammered tin, taken from olive-oil cans, old signs, and rusty billboards; they look like the tumbledown slums of the African quarters. It's not worth looking inside—not worth it, and not really the sort of thing one does.

The crates of the wealthy stand in the main downtown streets or in the shadowy byways of exclusive neighborhoods. You can look at them and admire. The crates of the poor, on the other hand, languish in entranceways, in backyards, in sheds. They are hidden for the time being, but in the end they will have to be transported the length of the city to the port, and the thought of that pitiful display is unappetizing.

Thanks to the abundance of wood that has collected here in Luanda, this dusty desert city nearly devoid of trees now smells like a flourishing forest. It's as if the forest had suddenly taken root in the streets, the squares, and the plazas. In the evenings I throw the window open to take a deep breath of it, and the war fades. I no longer hear the moans of Dona Esmeralda, I no longer see the ruined playboy with his two pistols, and I feel just as if I were sleeping it off in a forester's cottage in Bory Tucholski.

The building of the wooden city, the city of crates, goes on day after day, from dawn to twilight. Everyone works, soaked with rain, burned by the sun; even the millionaires, if they are physically fit, turn to the task. The enthusiasm of the adults infects the children. They too build crates, for their dolls and toys. Packing takes place under cover of night. It's better that way, when no one's sticking his nose into other people's business, nobody's keeping track of who puts in how much and what (and everyone knows there are a lot of that sort around, the ones who serve the MPLA and can't wait to inform).

So by night, in the thickest darkness, we transfer the contents of the stone city to the inside of the wooden city. It takes a lot of effort and sweat, lifting and struggling, shoulders sore from stowing it all, knees sore from squeezing it all in because it all has to fit and, after all, the stone city was big and the wooden city is small.

Gradually, from night to night, the stone city lost its value in favor of the wooden city. Gradually too, it changed in people's estimation. People stopped thinking in terms of houses and apartments and discussed only crates. Instead of saying, "I've got to go see what's at home," they said, "I've got to go check my crate." By now that was the only thing that interested them, the only thing they cared about. The Luanda they were leaving had become a stiff and alien stage set, empty, for the show was over.

Nowhere else in the world had I seen such a city, and I may never see anything like it again. It existed for months, and then it suddenly began disappearing. Or rather, quarter after quarter, it was taken on trucks to the port. Now it was spread out at the very edge of the sea, illuminated at night by harbor lanterns and the glare of lights on anchored ships. By day, people wound through its chaotic streets, painting their names and addresses on little plates, just as anyone does anywhere in the world when he builds himself a house. You could convince yourself, therefore, that this is a normal wooden town, except that it's been closed up by its residents who, for unknown reasons, have had to leave it in haste.

But afterward, when things had already turned very bad in the stone city and we, its handful of inhabitants, were waiting like desperadoes for the day of its destruction, the wooden city sailed away on the ocean. It was carried off by a great flotilla with which, after several hours, it disappeared below the horizon. This happened suddenly, as if a pirate fleet had sailed into the port, seized a priceless treasure, and escaped to sea with it.

Even so, I managed to see how the city sailed away. At dawn it was still rocking off the coast, piled up confusedly, uninhabited, lifeless, as if magically transformed into a museum exhibit of an ancient Eastern city and the last tour group had left. At that hour it was foggy and cold. I stood on the shore with some Angolan soldiers and a little crowd of ragtag freezing black children. "They've taken everything from us," one of the soldiers said without malice, and turned to cut a pineapple because that fruit, so overripe that, when it was cut, the juice ran out like water from a cup, was then our only food. "They've taken everything from us," he repeated and buried his face in the golden bowl of the fruit. The homeless harbor children gazed at him with greedy, fascinated eyes. The soldier lifted his juice-smeared face, smiled, and added, "But anyway, we've got a home now. They left us what's ours." He stood and, rejoicing in the thought that Angola was his, shot off a whole round from his automatic rifle into the air. Sirens sounded, seagulls darted and wheeled over the water, and the city stirred and began to sail away.

I don't know if there had ever been an instance of a whole city sailing across the ocean, but that is exactly what happened. The city sailed out into the world, in search of its inhabitants. These were the former residents of Angola, the Portuguese, who had scattered throughout Europe and America. A part of them reached South Africa. All fled Angola in haste, escaping before the conflagration of war, convinced that in this country there would be no more life and only the cemeteries would remain. But before they left they had still managed to build the wooden city in Luanda, into which they packed everything that had been in the stone city. On the streets now there were only thousands of cars, rusting and covered with dust. The walls also remained, the roofs, the asphalt on the roads, and the iron benches along the boulevards.

And now the wooden city was sailing on an Atlantic swept by violent, gale-driven waves. Somewhere on the ocean the partition of the city occurred and one section, the largest, sailed to Lisbon, the second to Rio de Janeiro, and the third to Capetown. Each of these sections reached its haven safely. I know this from various sources. Maria wrote to tell me that her crates ended up in Brazil—crates that had been part of the wooden city. Many newspapers wrote about the fact that one section made it to Capetown. And here's what I saw with my own eyes. After leaving Luanda, I stopped in Lisbon. A friend drove me along a wide street at the mouth of the Tagus, near the port. And there I saw fantastic heaps of crates stacked to perilous heights, unmoved, abandoned, as if they belonged to no one. This was the largest section of the wooden Luanda, which had sailed to the coast of Europe.

Back in the days when the erection of the wooden city had barely begun, the merchants had the biggest headaches. What could they do with the merchandise of all kinds that lay in the shops and filled the warehouses to their cobwebbed ceilings? No one could imagine a crate capable of accommodating the inventory of the leading wholesaler in Luanda, Don Castro Soremenho e Sousa. And the other wholesalers? And the thousand-strong clans of specialist retailers?

In addition, the whole import trade was behaving as if somebody was playing with less than a full deck. European firms—didn't anybody read the newspapers back there?—were shipping back-ordered merchandise to Luanda, oblivious of the fact that flames of armed conflagration were licking at Angola. Who now needed the complete sets of bathroom equipment shipped yesterday by Koenig and Sons GmbH, Hamburg? Who could suppress a chuckle at the arrival from London of an order of tennis balls, rackets, and golf clubs? As if for the sake of irony, a big shipment of insecticide sprayers came in from Marseilles—ordered by the very coffee planters now fighting for seats on flights to Europe.

Don Urbano Tavares, the proprietor of a jewelry shop on the main street, can feel content despite the mad unhappiness everywhere. When he chose his line of work years ago, he hit the bull's-eye. Gold always sells, and what's left fits easily into carry-on luggage. Lively action marks his business now. But not only gold is booming. People are rushing above all to food shops, because there is less and less to eat. Jostling crowds fill clothing and shoe stores. Watches and miniature radios, cosmetics and medicine are selling—small, light items that can be useful in the new life in countries beyond the sea.

A visit to a bookshop on Largo de Portugal leaves a sad impression. It is empty. Dust has settled in a gray layer on the old counter. Not a single customer. Who wants to read books now? The soldiers bought up the last pornographic magazines long ago and took them to the front. What's left—stacks of masterpieces mixed with the most second-rate reading matter—interests no one. Scribblers can draw an important lesson in modesty here. Immortal classics and page-turner romances are equally unattractive to the refugees for a simple reason: Paper is heavy.

A shop bearing the pious name Cruz de Cristo also stands empty. The specialty of the house is selling and renting wedding dresses. The owner, Dona Amanda, sits motionless for hours, unoccupied, among a crowd of similarly unmoving mute mannequins bewitched by some invisible fairy. There are enough dresses to furnish one of those mass weddings still popular in Mexico to this day. All white, right down to the ground, but each one cut differently, each one splendid in its baroque wealth of flounces and lace. What does Dona Amanda look forward to? One need only glance through the display window at her downcast, gloomy face. The time for joy and weddings has passed and left Dona Amanda surrounded by the unneeded props of an extinguished epoch.

Better luck (if that's the right word—I doubt it) attends Don Francisco Amarel Reis, owner of the Caminho ao Ceu (Road to Heaven) firm, concealed discreetly in a side street at the edge of the city center. His specialty: crosses, caskets, foil flowers, funeral accessories. These days there are many deaths, since fear, despair, and frustration lead people to the grave. There is a multitude of tragic automobile accidents here because the general atmosphere of rout, defeat, rage, and entrapment turns every susceptible driver into a beast. So we have funeral after funeral.

I am writing about people to whom Dona Cartagina introduced me. The old lady was the guardian spirit of the hotel and she wanted to arrange everything. She was the only person interested in Dona Amanda's gowns, because she was conjuring up a vision of the wedding of Maria and Arturo. She argued with Don Francisco about the cost of Dona Esmeralda's funeral, because Dona Esmeralda wouldn't come out of her coma. Only to the bookstore did I go alone, because I like to spend time in the company of books.

We buried Dona Esmeralda in a cemetery on a steep slope above the sea. The cemetery is as white as if covered by eternal snow. Needlelike cypresses, almost dark blue in the sunlight, shoot up heavenward out of the snow. The gate is painted blue, a warm and optimistic color in this case, suggesting that those who come here march heavenward like the saints in Louis Armstrong's song.

The next day Don Silva, the crotchety miser with the suit full of diamonds, left. Later I took Maria and Arturo to the airport.

Now several planes a day—French, Portuguese, Russian, and Italian—were flying. The pilots would get out and look around the airport. I watched them, amazed at the thought that only a few hours before they had been in Europe. I looked at them as at people from another planet. Europe—that was a distant, unreal point in a galaxy whose existence could be proved only by complicated deduction. They flew out in the evening. The overloaded machines crept to the runway, gained altitude with difficulty, and disappeared among the stars.

The nomad city without roofs and walls, the city of refugees around the airport, gradually vanished from the earth. At the same time, the wooden city deserted Luanda and waited in the port for its long journey. Of all the cities on the bay, only the stone Luanda, ever more depopulated and superfluous, remained.

That was the beginning of October. The city was becoming more desolate each day. Starting in the morning I wandered the streets without aim, without purpose, until the crushing heat drove me back to the hotel. At noon the sun beat against my head; it became so close and hot that there was nothing to breathe. Summer was beginning and the gates of a tropical hell were opening. Water was running short because the pumping stations were situated on the front lines, and after each repair they were destroyed again in the course of the fighting. I walked around dirty, needing something to drink so badly that I came down with a fever and saw orange spots before my eyes.

More and more merchants closed their shops. Black boys drummed with sticks on the lowered metal shutters. Restaurants and cafés were already out of action; chairs, tables, and folded umbrellas stood around on the sidewalks and afterward disappeared into the African slums. From time to time some car would drive through the empty streets, running the red lights that kept functioning automatically, God knows for whom.

At about this time, someone brought news to the hotel that all the police had left!

Now Luanda, of all the cities in the world, had no police. When you find yourself in such a situation, you feel strange. On the one hand everything seems light, loose, but on the other hand there is a certain uneasiness. The few whites who still wandered the city accepted the development with foreboding. Rumors circulated that the black quarters would descend upon the stone city. Everyone knew that the blacks lived in the most awful conditions, in the worst slums to be seen anywhere in Africa, in clay hovels like heaps of smashed cheap pottery covering the desert around Luanda. And here stood the luxurious stone city of glass and concrete—empty, no one's. If only they would come peacefully, in an orderly way, with their families, and occupy what was abandoned and vacant. But according to the terrified Portuguese who passed themselves off as experts on the native mentality, the blacks would burst in, swept up in a madness of destruction and hatred, drunk, drugged with secret herbs, demanding blood and revenge. Nothing could hold back that invasion. Exhausted people with shattered nerves, unarmed and at bay, talk and dream up the most apocalyptic visions. Everyone is lost and it will be the most hideous death—stabbed to death in the streets, hacked with machetes on their own doorsteps. Those with more presence of mind propose various kinds of self-defense. One says to extinguish all the lights and keep watch in the darkened city. Another says the opposite: Turn on the lights even in empty houses, because only numbers, massed numbers, will be able to scare off the blacks. As usual, no argument prevails and at night the city looks like a curtain full of holes—here a fragment of some scene shines through, then around it nothing can be seen, then there's another fragment, then everything is covered. Dona Cartagina, who more from habit than necessity is cleaning the vacant rooms on my floor (I'm all alone there now), pauses in her sweeping to listen for the sinister rumble of a crowd, the harbinger of our doom, approaching from the black quarters. She freezes just like a village woman in the field listening for thunder. Then she crosses herself solemnly and goes on cleaning.

All the firemen have left! Now no one will save the city from fires. At first, people cannot believe that the firemen have deserted their posts, but to convince themselves they have only to visit the main engine company on the shorefront boulevard. The gates of the station are standing open. Inside sit the big red-and-gold fire engines with ladders and hoses. The firemen's helmets sit on shelves. There isn't a living soul. Of course the FNLA will find out about this, and all it will take is one bomb dropped tomorrow in place of the leaflets. All Luanda will go up like a matchbox. The rains have stopped, the city is sun-baked and dry as sawdust. If only there isn't a short circuit, if only some drunk doesn't get careless. Later the soldiers get one of the pumpers running and use it to carry water to the front. Since it is easy to spot from a distance, it is hit, runs into a ditch, and stays there.

All the garbagemen have left!

At first, nobody noticed. The city was dirty and neglected, so people assumed that the garbagemen had flown to Europe a long time ago. Then it turned out that they had left only the day before. Suddenly, no one knew from where, the garbage started piling up. After all, there was only a handful of residents left and they were so apathetic and inert that no one could accuse them of carrying out such mountains of garbage. Yet mounds of it began piling up on the streets of the abandoned city. It appeared on the sidewalks, in the roads, in the squares, in the entranceways of townhouses, and in the extinct marketplaces. You could walk through some streets only with great effort and disgust. In this climate the excess of sun and moisture accelerate and intensify decay, rot, and fermentation. The whole city began to stink, and anybody who had a long walk through the streets to his hotel picked up that stench, too, and other people spoke to him from a distance. In general, people distanced themselves from each other even though, in the situation to which we were condemned, it should have been the other way around. Dona Cartagina closed all the windows because the putrid air that blew in was unbreathable. The cats started dying. They must have poisoned themselves collectively on some carrion, because one morning dead cats were lying everywhere. After two days they puffed up and swelled to the size of piglets. Black flies swarmed over them. The odor was unbearable. I walked through the city dripping with sweat, holding a handkerchief to my nose. Dona Cartagina said the prayers against pestilence. There were no doctors, and not a single hospital or pharmacy remained open. The garbage grew and multiplied like the rising of a monstrous, disgusting dough expanding in all directions, impelled by a poisonous deadly yeast.

Later, when all the barbers, repairmen, mail carriers, and concierges had left, the stone city lost its reason for existing, its sense. It was like a dry skeleton polished by the wind, a dead bone sticking up out of the ground toward the sun.

The dogs were still alive.

They were pets, abandoned by owners fleeing in panic. You could see dogs of all the most expensive breeds, without masters—boxers, bulldogs, greyhounds, Dobermans, dachshunds, Airedales, spaniels, even Scotch terriers and Great Danes, pugs and poodles. Deserted, stray, they roamed in a great pack looking for food. As long as the Portuguese army was there, the dogs gathered every morning on the square in front of the general headquarters and the sentries fed them canned NATO rations. It was like watching an international pedigreed dog show. Afterward the fed, satisfied pack moved to the soft, juicy mowed grass on the lawn of the Government Palace. An unlikely mass sex orgy began, excited and indefatigable madness, chasing and tumbling to the point of utter abandon. It gave the bored sentries a lot of ribald amusement.

When the army left, the dogs began to go hungry and slim down. For a while they drifted around the city in a desultory mob, looking for a handout. One day they disappeared. I think they followed the human example and left Luanda, since I never came across a dead dog afterward, though hundreds of them had been loitering in front of the general headquarters and frolicking in front of the palace. One could suppose that an energetic leader emerged from the ranks to take the pack out of the dying city. If the dogs went north, they ran into the FNLA. If they went south, they ran into UNITA. On the other hand, if they went east, in the direction of Nda-latando and Saurimo, they might have made it into Zambia, then to Mozambique or even Tanzania.

Perhaps they're still roaming, but I don't know in what direction or in what country.

After the exodus of the dogs, the city fell into rigor mortis. So I decided to go to the front.

Part II

Part II

Commandante Ndozi stands in the shade of a spreading mango tree. He wipes his sweaty face. Winning a battle takes physical exertion, too. It is just like cutting down a forest. He orders a group of soldiers to bury the dead. Friend and foe can be interred together—nothing means anything after death. Besides, as our proverb has it: Enemies on earth, brothers in heaven. He asks if the truck has left for Luanda with the wounded. It hasn't, because the driver is waiting for a shipment of gasoline. The wounded are lying in the truck, moaning and calling for help. There is no doctor on this front. If the gasoline doesn't come, half the wounded will bleed to death. Then Ndozi sends an orderly in the direction of some gunfire. He is to see if it is a skirmish with the withdrawing enemy, or if the boys are firing salutes to celebrate the victory. He suspects they are wasting ammunition, which is also running short. The enemy will strike tomorrow and we will give up the town because there won't be anything to defend it with. He says he has eternal problems with ammunition. Eternal—that's stretching it. This is the beginning of the war and his unit has only been in existence for a month.

Ndozi has years of guerrilla warfare behind him, but

the troops he is leading are green. A green soldier fears everything. When he is transported to the front, he thinks death is watching him on every side. Every shot is aimed at him. He doesn't know how to judge the range or direction of fire, so he shoots anywhere, as long as he can shoot a lot without stopping. He is not hurting the enemy, he is killing his own terror. He is stifling the dread that paralyzes a man and prevents him from thinking. Or rather, the dread doesn't let him think about what is happening around him, about how to win the battle that his unit is engaged in, because at that moment he has a more important battle to win: He must win the war with his own fear. During the attack today, says Ndozi, I ran up to one who was standing there shooting a bazooka straight up in the air. Don't aim up, I screamed, aim in front of you at those palms, that's where they are. But I could see that he had a gray face, that finding the enemy hadn't crossed his mind, that nothing was getting through to him because he was fighting his own enemy, who wasn't among the palms but inside him, in the boy himself. He was firing because he wanted to stun himself, he wanted to stupefy himself and survive the attack of fear.

Ndozi continues his account. The supply officers call: Who did you share your ammunition with? I answer that it's been fired. How many did you kill? Two. A half ton of cartridges and only two dead? But there was no need to kill more; we were to take the town, and we've taken it. None of the quartermasters comes to the front to see how green soldiers, who don't know war, fight. At night, the unit moves up close to where the enemy is. We open fire just before dawn. The inexperienced soldier thinks the main thing is to make a big racket. He fires like a man possessed, blindly, because all he cares about is noise, communicating to the enemy how much strength is approaching. This is a form of warning, a way of evoking a fear in the opponent that will be greater than ours. And there is a sort of rationale to it. Because the other side is also unfamiliar with war, unfamiliar with gunfire; surprised by the volley, they withdraw and flee.

The skirmishes in the first days of the war were limited to just such auctions of firepower. They rarely came to direct combat. Once, says Ndozi, I lived through such an adventure: My people shot off all their ammunition at the beginning and later they couldn't attack because there was nothing to attack with. I sent scouts into the town that we were supposed to attack. They returned and said that there wasn't a soul there, the enemy had fled. When we walked into our objective, nobody in my unit had a single cartridge in his clip.

We didn't want this war, Ndozi insists. But Holden Roberto struck from the north and Jonas Savimbi from the south. This country has been at war for five hundred years, ever since the Portuguese came. They needed slaves for trade, for export to Brazil and the Caribbean and across the ocean generally. Of all Africa, Angola supplied the greatest number of slaves to those countries. That's why they call our country the Black Mother of the New World. Half the Brazilian, Cuban, and Dominican peasants are descended from Angolans. This was once a populous, settled country and then it was emptied, as if there'd been a plague. Angola is empty to this day. Hundreds of kilometers and not a single person, like in the Sahara. The slave wars went on for three hundred years or more. It was good business for our chiefs. The strong tribes attacked the weak, took prisoners, and put them on the market. Sometimes they had to do it, to pay the Portuguese taxes. The price of a slave was fixed according to the quality of his teeth. People pulled out their teeth or ground them away with stones in order to have a lower market value. So much suffering to be free. From generation to generation, tribes lived in fear of each other, they lived in hatred. The military campaigns took place in the dry season, because it was easier to move then. When the rains ended, everyone knew that the times of misfortune and of hunting for people had begun. In the rainy season, when the country was drowning in water and mud, hostilities stopped. But the chiefs were thinking up new campaigns, marshaling new forces. This is remembered by everyone even today because, in our thinking, the past takes up more space than the future.

I began fighting ten years ago, says Ndozi, in Commandante Batalho's unit. That was eastern Angola. We had to learn the languages of the local tribes and act in accordance with their customs. This was a condition of survival—otherwise, they would have treated us as foreigners trespassing on their land. And yet, we were all Angolans. But they don't know that this country is called Angola. For them, the land ends at the last village where the people speak a language they understand. That's the border of their world. But, we asked, what lies beyond that border? Beyond that border lies another planet inhabited by the Nganguela, which means nonhumans. You have to keep an eye on those Nganguelas, because there are a lot of them and they use an incomprehensible language that conceals their evil designs.

All our enemies feed on the backwardness of the people, he says, and pay handsomely to keep the tribal wars going without end. They bought Holden Roberto so he'd create the FNLA from the Bakonga. They bought Savimbi to create UNITA from the Ovimbundi. We have a hundred tribes and must build one nation out of them. How long will it take? Nobody knows. We have to wean the people from hatred. We have to introduce the custom of shaking hands.

This is an unlucky country, he continues, just as there are unlucky people whose lives just don't want to work out. The Portuguese were constantly organizing armed expeditions to conquer all Angola over the last two hundred years. There's been no peace. We've been fighting a guerrilla war for fifteen years. No country in Africa has had such a long war. None has been so devastated. There were never many of us guerrillas. Then some died and others left for headquarters or the government. Only a handful of the old cadres remained at the front. We are scattered all over the country. We are short of people.

The troops with me are boys taken straight from the streets to the front. They ought to be in school, but we closed the schools in order to have an army, since we have to defend ourselves. This war was forced on us because we are a rich country inhabited by five million poor people, benighted illiterates incapable of operating an 86-mm recoilless rifle. The other side thinks it'll only take twenty armored vehicles to go on having our oil and diamonds and to put us back in our place. They didn't give us time for anything, we have green troops who have to grow up to fight. For me, it's a waste of these boys because they ought to grow up to read and write, to build towns and make people healthy. But they have to grow up to kill. They have to grow up to having less and less blind shooting on our side and more and more death on the other side. What other way out do we have in this war that we never wanted?

I am in Caxito, over sixty kilometers north of Luanda. Commandante Ju-Ju telephoned this morning to say there had been a battle for Caxito at dawn, that Commandante Ndozi's unit had seized the town from the FNLA and it would be possible to go there presently. Ju-Ju is the political commissar of the MPLA general staff and he reads a communiqué on the war situation over the radio at eight each evening. These communiqués sound high-flown because Ju-Ju puts his heart and soul into them. One day we are weeping over the death of the late lamented Commandante Cowboy, who fell in the assault on the town of Ngavi. The intrepid hero refused to take cover and, severely wounded, dealt out death to three bestial aggressors. The next day we are celebrating the triumph at Folgares, where our glory-bedecked army delivered a shattering blow to a band of venal mercenaries. On another occasion we learn that all Africa is following with bated breath the fate of the heroic garrison in Luso, which has resolved to yield not an inch of ground to the numberless horde surrounding it. Our spirit will never weaken, our will to fight is inflexible as steel, we do not know fear, we do not fear death, and we are perishing in the eyes of an admiring world.

Ju-Ju's communiqués are brief and calm when things are going well. The facts speak for themselves, and you don't have to beg people to back a winner. But when something turns rotten, when it starts going bad, the communiqués become prolix and crabbed, adjectives proliferate, and self-praise and epithets scorning the enemy multiply. Ju-Ju's voice reaches out to me through open windows as I walk the streets of Luanda. At this distance I can't make out the words, but the fact that he talks for only a moment tells me that it's good, that they are holding out, that they have taken something. But yesterday I covered half the city while Ju-Ju went on and on. Something had obviously gone wrong at the front. A thousand doubts descended on me: Would they manage to stick it out? Would they win?

Ju-Ju is a white Angolan, which means that his family comes from Portugal but he was born in Angola, which is his homeland. There are hundreds like him in the MPLA. They fight at the front or work in the staff or in administration. They all wear beards. That is a mark of identity here: A white with a beard is from Angola and nobody asks for his documents or pulls him in for interrogation. The blacks call him "*camarada*" and treat him with respect, because if he's a white with a beard he must be somebody, the leader of a unit or higher. Ju-Ju has a beard like a Byzantine patriarch—down to his chest, impressive. That beard is the most striking thing about him, because he is small, thin, and stooped; he wears thick glasses and resembles a lecturer in the department of classical languages at one of the older European universities.

During the conquest of Caxito, Commandante Ndozi's unit took 120 FNLA prisoners; Ju-Ju is interrogating them. They are summoned one by one under a large chestnut tree, where the political commissar is seated on an ammunition crate (grenades, French manufacture, captured from the enemy). By nature a shy man, Ju-Ju speaks politely or even deferentially to each of them and concludes the conversation by imparting a lesson, in the hope that it will lead the prisoner into the correct road of life and endeavor. He begins by evoking feelings of shame and guilt in his subject.

"Aren't you ashamed," the political commissar asks, "to be fighting in the FNLA as an agent of imperialism?"

A glum, vacant-looking Bakongo with skin so black that it shades toward violet, and a mug ugly enough to make your flesh crawl, says nothing and stares at the ground. He adjusts a bloody rag tied around his head where a bullet has taken one of his ears off. He sighs and seems ready to cry, but still says nothing.

Ju-Ju encourages him to talk, insists, even offers him a cigarette, although cigarettes are a priceless treasure in Angola and you can save your life for a pack or even half.

The prisoner answers at last that in Kinshasa (in Zaïre) they make roundups of Angolan Bakongos and press-gang them into the FNLA. Mobutu's troops conduct these roundups. Whoever has the francs can buy his way out, but he didn't have the francs because he was unemployed, so when they caught him they press-ganged him. It was good in the FNLA because they gave you something to eat. They give you manioc and lamb. On Saturdays they give you beer. If you win a battle, you get money. But he wasn't in any battles they got paid for. He stole nothing, because everything was already looted and empty from the Zaïrian border to Caxito. He never saw Holden Roberto. He doesn't know how to read and write. They were surrounded this morning, so they surrendered and here they are. He didn't kill anybody.

Ju-Ju orders the next one brought in: a Bakongo with hair that begins right above his eyebrows, reeling in terror. The commissar asks if he isn't ashamed, etc., then asks where the nearest FNLA troops are.

This one doesn't know. It was so mixed up that he doesn't know who was captured and who got away. One mercenary shouted at him, "That way, that way," and he obeyed and ran right into the MPLA, while the mercenary took off in the other direction and escaped. Among his fellow prisoners, he knows nobody. He and four others were sent from Ambriz to Caxito. They had nothing to eat or drink, because there is nothing on that road. Three died of exhaustion. One disappeared at night. He was left alone. He arrived in Caxito last evening. He wants to drink. He thinks that if there are any FNLA nearby, they will give up tomorrow on their own because there is no water in the vicinity except in Caxito. They will hold out overnight and perhaps until noon, then they will come in because otherwise they'll die of thirst.

The next prisoner looks twelve. He says he's sixteen. He knows it is shameful to fight for the FNLA, but they told him that if he went to the front they would send him to school afterward. He wants to finish school because he wants to paint. If he could get paper and a pencil he could draw something right now. He could do a portrait. He also knows how to sculpt and would like to show his sculptures, which he left in Carmona. He has put his whole life into it and would like to study, and they told him that he will, if he goes to the front first. He knows how it works—in order to paint you must first kill people, but he hasn't killed anyone.

It was dark by the time I walked out into the square. Empty houses, no lights, windows broken, smashed shops. Some dogs near the well. Nobody's cow, with its nose in the grass.

The front.

The dark wall of bush on all sides, and in the bush perhaps those FNLA soldiers who won't hold out long without water and will give up tomorrow if they don't die of thirst.

A dead little town, overwhelming emptiness and night. There are voices, conversations, and even laughter in only one place, at the other end of the square. Over there, where there is a small wall surrounded by a concrete balustrade, with a clump of trees in the middle. I walked toward the yard, stumbling over stones, artillery shells, an abandoned bicycle.

The FNLA prisoners, the 120 captured this morning during the battle for Caxito, stood along the inside of the balustrade. Along the outside, in the street and the square, stood MPLA sentries. There were a dozen or so of them.

Prisoners and guards were carrying on a lively conversation, arguing over the result of yesterday's soccer match. Yesterday, Sunday, Benfica defeated Ferroviario 2–1 at the stadium in Luanda. Ferroviario, which had not lost in two years, left the field to the boos of its own fans. The team lost because its premier striker and league-leading scorer, Chico Gordo, had left his club to play for Sporting de Braga in Portugal.

They could have won.

No way.

Chico Gordo—so what! Norberto's just as good! But they lost anyway.

Norberto? Norberto isn't fit to carry Chico's shoes.

Divided into two camps, ready to leap at each other's throats, the boys wrangle and debate. Except that the dividing line doesn't run along the concrete balustrade. Ferroviario has fans among both prisoners and guards. And in the other camp, the camp of the Benfica fans celebrating their splendid triumph, there are also both prisoners and guards. It is a fervent argument, full of youthful passion, like the ones you can see anywhere in the world among boys leaving the stadium after a big game. In this kind of discussion you forget about everything.

And it's good that you can forget about everything. That you can forget about that battle, after which there were fewer of us on both sides of the balustrade. About the roundups that Mobutu's soldiers carry out. And about how we have to grow up to war, so that there will be less and less blind shooting and more and more death.

Part III

For a long time now, I've been making expeditions to the general staff to secure a pass for the southern front. Moving around the country without a pass is impossible because checkpoints for the inspection of travel documents stand guard along the roads. There is usually a checkpoint on the way into each town and another one on the way out, but as you drive through villages you may also run across checkpoints thrown up by wary and vigilant peasants; at times a checkpoint spontaneously established by nomads grazing their herds nearby will appear in the middle of an open field or in the most untenanted bush.

On important routes where major checkpoints are found, the road is blocked by colorful barriers that can be seen from a distance. But since materials are scarce and improvisation is the rule, others do the best they can. Some stretch a cable at the height of a car's windshield, and if they don't have cable they use a length of sisal rope. They stand empty gasoline drums in the road or erect obstacles of stones and volcanic boulders. They scatter glass and nails on the macadam. They lay down dry thorn branches. They barricade the way with wreaths of stapelia or with cycad trunks. The most inventive people, it turns out, are the ones from the checkpoint at Mulando. From a roadside inn abandoned by a Portuguese, they dragged into the middle of the road a ceiling-high wardrobe built in the form of a huge triptych with a movable crystal-glass mirror mounted on the central section. By manipulating this mirror so that it reflected the rays of the sun, they blinded drivers who, unable to proceed, stopped a good distance off and walked to the checkpoint to explain who they were and where they were going.

You have to learn how to live with the checkpoints and to respect their customs, if you want to travel without hindrance and reach your destination alive. It must be borne in mind that the fate of our expedition, and even our lives, are in the hands of the sentries. These are people of diverse professions and ages. Rear-guard soldiers, homegrown militia, boys caught up in the passion of war, and often simply children. The most varied armament: submachine guns, old carbines, machetes, knives, and clubs. Optional dress, because uniforms are hard to come by. Sometimes a military blouse, but usually a resplendent shirt; sometimes a helmet, but often a woman's hat; sometimes massive boots, but as a rule sneakers or bare feet. This is an indigent war, attired in cheap calico.

Every encounter with a checkpoint consists of: (a) the explanatory section, (b) bargaining, (c) friendly conversation. You have to drive up to the checkpoint slowly and stop at a decent remove. Any violent braking or squealing of tires constitutes a bad opening; the sentries don't appreciate such stunts. Next we get out of the car and approach the barriers, gasoline drums, heaps of stones, tree trunks, or wardrobe. If this is a zone near the front, our legs buckle with fear and our heart is in our mouth, because we can't tell whose checkpoint it is—the MPLA's, FNLA's, or UNITA's. The sun is shining and it's hot. Air heated to whiteness vibrates above the road, as if a snowdrift were billowing across the pavement. But it's quiet, and an unmoving world, holding its breath, surrounds us. We too, involuntarily, hold our breath.

We stop and wait. There is no one in sight.

But the sentries are there. Concealed in the bushes or in a roadside hut, they are watching us intently. We're exposed to their gaze and, God forbid, to their fire. At such a moment you can't show either nervousness or haste, because both will end badly. So we act normal, correct, relaxed: We just wait. Nor will it help to go to the other extreme and mask fear with an artificial casualness, or joke around, show off, or display an exaggerated self-confidence. The sentries might infer that we are treating them lightly and the results could be catastrophic. Nor do they like it when travelers put their hands in their pockets, look around, lie down in the shade of the nearby trees, or—this is generally considered a crime—themselves set about removing the obstacles from the road.

At the conclusion of the observation period, the people from the checkpoint leave their hiding places and walk in our direction in a slow, lazy step, but alert and with their weapons at the ready. They stop at a safe distance.

The strangers stay where they are.

Remember that the sun is shining and it's hot.

Now begins the most dramatic moment of the encounter: mutual examination. To understand this scene, we must bear in mind that the armies fighting each other are dressed (or undressed) alike and that large regions of the country are no-man's-land into which first one side and then the other penetrates and sets up checkpoints. That is why, at first, we don't know who these people are or what they will do with us.

Now we have to summon up all our courage to say one word, which will determine our life or death: "*Camarada!*"

If the sentries are Agostinho Neto's people, who salute each other with the word *camarada*, we will live. But if they turn out to be Holden Roberto's or Jonas Savimba's people, who call each other *irmão* (brother), we have reached the limit of our earthly existence. In no time they will put us to work—digging our own graves. In front of the old, established checkpoints there are little cemeteries of those who had the misfortune to greet the sentries with the wrong word.

But let's say that fortune has smiled on us this time. We have announced ourselves with *camarada* in a voice strangled and hoarsened by fear. The word has been enunciated in such a way that some sort of sound will reach the people at the checkpoint, but not an overly distinct, overly literal, and irrevocable sound: Our mumbling, into which we have cautiously smuggled the fragile syllables of the word *camarada*, will thus leave us with a loophole, a chance of reversing, of retreating into the word *irmão*, so that the unhappy confusion of words can be blamed on the hellish heat that dulls and addles the mind, on the exhaustion of travel, and the nervousness understandable in anyone who finds himself at the front. This is a delicate game; it demands skill, tact, and a good ear. Any taking the easy way out, any heavy-handedness, shows immediately. We can't, for instance, shout *"Camarada! Irmão!"* all at once, unless we want to be regarded—and rightly so—as the kind of opportunists who are scorned in front-line situations all over the world. We will arouse their suspicion and be held for interrogation.

So we have said *"Camarada!"* and the faces of the people from the checkpoint brighten. They answer *"Camarada!"* Everybody begins repeating *"Camarada! Camarada!"* sportively and loudly an unending number of times as the word circulates between us and the sentries like a flock of doves.

The euphoria that sweeps over us at the thought that we will live does not last long, however. We will live, but whether we will continue our journey is still an open question. So we proceed to the first, explanatory part of the meeting. We tell who we are, where we are headed, and where we are coming from. At exactly this moment we present our pass. Troubles arise if the sentry can't read—an epidemic problem in the case of peasant and nomad sentries. The better-organized checkpoints employ children to this end. Children know how to read more often than adults, because schools have begun to develop only in the last few years. The contents of a general staff pass are usually warm and friendly. They state that *Camarada* Ricardo Kapuchinsky is our friend, a man of good will, reliable, and all *camaradas* at the front and in the rear are therefore asked to show him hospitality and assist him.

Despite such a positive recommendation, the people from the checkpoint begin as a rule by saying that they don't want us to go on and order us to turn back. This is understandable. True, the authority of Luanda is

49

great—but then, doesn't the checkpoint also constitute authority? And the essence of authority is that it must manifest its power.

But let's not give up hope or become dispirited! Let's reach into the arsenal of persuasion. A thousand arguments speak in our favor. We have our documents in order: There is the text, the stamp, and the signature. We know President Agostinho Neto personally. We know the front commander. We are writing dispatches, we are making Angola and its champions of right famous around the world. The bad Europeans have decamped and whoever stayed must be on their side or he wouldn't have stuck it out. Finally: Search us—we have no weapons, we can't harm anybody.

Slowly, stubbornly, the sentries yield. They talk it over, they confer off to one side, and sometimes a quarrel breaks out among them. They can send a message to their commander, who has driven to the city or set out for a village. Then we have to wait. Wait and wait, which we spend our whole life here doing. But this has its good side, since shared waiting leads to mutual familiarity and closeness. We have already become a particle of the checkpoint society. If there is time and interest, we can tell them something about Poland. We have a sea and mountains of our own. We have forests, but the trees are different: There isn't a single baobab in Poland. Coffee doesn't grow there, either. It is a smaller country than Angola, yet we have more people. We speak Polish. The Ovimbundi speak their own language, the Chokwe speak theirs, and we speak ours. We don't eat manioc; people in Poland don't know what manioc is. Everybody has shoes. You can go barefoot there only in the summer. In winter a barefoot person could get frostbite and die. Die from going barefoot? Ha! Ha! Is it far to Poland? Far, but close by airplane. And by sea it takes a month. A month? That's not far. Do we have rifles? We have rifles, artillery, and tanks. We have cattle just like here. Cows and goats, not so many goats. And haven't you ever seen a horse? Well, one of these days you'll have to see a horse. We have a lot of horses.

The time passes in agreeable conversation, which is exactly the way the sentries like it. Because people rarely dare to travel now. The roads are empty and you can go days without seeing a new face. And yet you can't complain of boredom. Life centers around the checkpoints these days, as in the Middle Ages it centered around the church. The local marketwomen set out their wares on scraps of linen: meaty bananas, hen's eggs as tiny as walnuts, red pili-pili, dried corn, black beans, and tart pomegranates. Clothing-stall owners sell the cheapest garments, garish scarves, and also wooden combs, plastic stars, pocket mirrors with the likenesses of known actresses on the back, rubber elephants, and fifes with keys that move. Any children not on active duty play in homespun shirts in the neighboring fields. You can encounter village women with clay jugs on their heads on their way to get water, walking from who knows where to who knows where.

The checkpoint, if composed of friendly people, is a hospitable stopping place. Here we can drink water and, sometimes, purchase a couple of liters of gasoline. We can get roast meat. If it's late, they let us sleep over. At times they have information about who controls the next stretch of road.

The time to leave approaches, and the sentries go to work. They open the road—they roll away the drums, push away the stones, move the wardrobe. And afterward, when we're about to drive off, they walk up to us with the one universally repeated question: Do we have any cigarettes?

Then there is a momentary reversal of roles. Authority passes into our hands because we, not they, have cigarettes. We decide whether they get one, two, or five cigarettes. Our sentries put down their weapons and wait obediently and patiently, with humility in their eyes. Let's be human about it and share evenly with them. They're in a war, fighting and risking their lives. Once the cigarettes are bestowed on them, they raise their hands in the victory sign, smile—and among shouts of "Camarada! Camarada!" we set out along the road into the unknown, into the empty world, into the mad, white scorching heat, into the fear that awaits us at the next checkpoint.

Roving thus from checkpoint to checkpoint, in an alternating rhythm of dread and joy, I reached Benguela. The road from Luanda to Benguela passes through six hundred kilometers of desert terrain, flat and nondescript. A haphazard medley of stones, frumpy dry bushes, dirty sand, and broken road signs creates a gray and incoherent landscape. In the rainy season the clouds churn right above the ground here, showers drag on for hours, and there is so little light in the air that day might as well not exist, only dusk and night. Even during heat waves, despite the excess of sun, the countryside resembles deserted, burned-out ruins: It is ashy, dead, and unsettling. People who must travel through here make haste in order to get the frightening vacancy behind them and arrive with relief at their destination, the oasis, as quickly as possible. Luanda is an oasis and Benguela is an oasis in this desert that stretches all along the coast of Angola.

Benguela: a sleepy, almost depopulated city slumbering in the shade of acacias, palms, and kipersols. The villa neighborhoods are empty, the houses locked up and drowned in flowers. Indescribable residential luxury, a dizzying excess of floor space and, in the streets before the gates, orphaned cars—Chevrolets and Alfa Romeos and Jaguars, probably in running order although nobody tries to drive them. And nearby, a hundred meters away, the desert—white and glimmering like a salt spill, without a blade of grass, without a single tree, beyond redemption. In this desert lie African settlements stuck together lackadaisically with clay and dung, hammered out of plywood and tin, swarming, stuffy, and miserable. Although the two worlds—comfort and poverty—stand only steps apart and no one is guarding the rich European neighborhood, the blacks from the clay huts haven't tried to move in. The idea hasn't crossed their minds. This might be the best explanation of their passive attitude. Because moral scruples don't come into play here, nor a fear that the whites will return and avenge themselves. These considerations might have been weighed, had they been tempted to take over the white quarters. But in these people's lives, the degree of consciousness that drives one to demand justice or do something about obtaining it hasn't yet been reached. Only those Africans who have acquired a university education, who have learned to read, got out into the world, and seen films—only they understand that decolonization has created a chance for rapid material advancement, for accumulating wealth and privileges. And taking advantage of the chance has come easily to them precisely because their less enlightened brothers—who are a dime a dozen—demand nothing for themselves, accepting their clay hut and bowl of manioc as the only world they will ever know or desire.

I spent some time walking the border of the two quarters, and then I went downtown. I found the lane in which the central-front staff was quartered in a spacious two-story villa. In front of the gate sat a guard with a face monstrously swollen by periostitis, groaning and squeezing his head, obviously terrified that his skull would burst. There was no way to communicate with such an unfortunate; nothing existed for him at that point. I opened the gate. In the garden, boxes of ammunition, mortar barrels, and piles of canteens lay on the flowerbeds in the shade of flaming bougainvilleas. Farther on, soldiers were sleeping side by side on the veranda and in the hall. I went upstairs and opened a door. There was nothing but a desk inside, and at the desk sat a large, powerfully built white man: Commandante Monti, the commander of the front.

He was typing a request to Luanda for people and weapons. The only armored personnel carrier he had at the front had been knocked out the day before by a mercenary. If the enemy attacked now with their own armored personnel carrier, he would have to give ground and retreat.

Monti read the letter that I had brought him from Luanda, ordered me to sit down—on the windowsill, because there were no chairs—and went on typing. A quarter of an hour later there were footsteps on the stairs and four people came in, a television crew from Lisbon.

They had come here for two days and afterward they would return to Portugal in their plane. The leader of the crew was Luis Alberto, a dynamic and restless mulatto, sharp and gusty. We immediately became friends. Monti and Alberto knew each other from way back, since they both came from Angola and perhaps even from right here in Benguela. So we didn't have to waste any time making introductions and getting to know one another.

Alberto and I wanted to drive to the front, but the rest of the crew—Carvalho, Fernandez, and Barbosa—were against it. They said they had wives and children, they had begun building houses outside Lisbon (near Cascais, a truly beautiful spot), and they weren't going to die in this mad, senseless war in which nobody knew anything, the opponents couldn't tell each other apart until the last second, and you could be blown away without any fighting, simply because of the crazy screwups, the lack of information, the laziness and callousness of blacks for whom human life had no value.

In other words, they expressed a desire to live.

A discussion began, which is what Latins love most of all. Alberto tried to sell them on the argument that they would shoot a lot of tape and make a lot of the money they all needed so badly. But it was Monti who finally assuaged them by saying that at that time of day—it was almost noon—there was no fighting on the front. And he gave the most straightforward explanation in the world: "It's too hot."

Outside the window the air was rippling like tin in a forge; every movement demanded effort. We started getting ready to hit the road. Monti went downstairs, woke up one of the soldiers, and sent him into town where, somewhere, there were drivers and cars. A Citroën DS and a Ford Mustang turned up. Monti wanted to make it nice for us, so as our escort he designated a soldier named Carlotta.

Carlotta came with an automatic on her shoulder. Even though she was wearing a commando uniform that was too big for her, you could tell she was attractive. We all started paying court to her immediately. In fact, it was Carlotta's presence that persuaded the crew to forget about their houses outside Lisbon and travel to the front. Only twenty years old, Carlotta was already a legend. Two months earlier, during the uprising in Huambo, she had led a small MPLA detachment that was surrounded by a thousand-strong UNITA force. She managed to break the encirclement and lead her people out. Girls generally make excellent soldiers—better than boys, who sometimes behave hysterically and irresponsibly at the front. Our girl was a mulatto with an elusive charm and, as it seemed to us then, great beauty. Later, when I developed the pictures of her, the only pictures of Carlotta that remained, I saw that she wasn't so beautiful. Yet nobody said as much out loud, so as not to destroy our myth, our image of Carlotta from that October afternoon in Benguela. I simply looked up Alberto, Carvalho, Fernandez, and Barbosa and showed them the pictures of Carlotta taken on the way to the front. They looked at them in silence and I think we all chose silence so we wouldn't have to comment on the subject of good looks. Did it mean anything in the end? Carlotta was gone by then. She had received an order to report to the front staff, so she put on her uniform, combed out her Afro, slung the automatic over her shoulder, and left. When Commandante Monti, four Portuguese, and a Pole saw her in front of staff headquarters, she seemed beautiful. Why? Because that was the kind of mood we were in, because we needed it, because we wanted it that way. We always create the beauty of women, and that day we created Carlotta's beauty. I can't explain it any other way.

The cars moved out and drove along the road to Balombo, 160 kilometers to the east. To tell the truth, we all should have died on the winding road, full of switchbacks that the drivers took like madmen; it was a miracle that we got there alive. Carlotta sat beside the driver in our car and, since she was used to that kind of driving, she kidded us a little. The force of the wind threw her head back, and Barbosa said he would hold on to Carlotta's head so the wind wouldn't tear it off. Carlotta laughed, and we envied Barbosa. At one of the stops, Fernandez proposed that Carlotta move to the back with us and sit on our knees, but she refused. We rejoiced out loud at his defeat. After all, Fernandez had clearly wanted Carlotta to sit on his own lap, which would have ruined everything since she didn't belong to anyone and we were creating her together, our Carlotta.

She was born in Roçadas, not far from the border of Namibia. She received her military training a year ago in the Kabinda forest. She wants to become a nurse after the war. That's all we know about this girl who is now riding in the car holding an automatic on her knees, and who, since we have run out of jokes and calmed down for a moment, has become serious and thoughtful. We know that Carlotta won't be Alberto's or Fernandez's, but we don't yet know that she will never again be anybody's.

We have to stop again because a bridge is damaged and the drivers have to figure out how to get across. We have a few minutes, so I take a picture of her. I ask her to smile. She stands leaning against the bridge railing. Around us lie fields, meadows perhaps—I don't remember.

After a while we drove on. We passed a burned-out village, an empty town, abandoned pineapple and tobacco plantations. Then a profusion of tamarisk shrubs that evolved into a forest. It got worse, because we were driving to the front on a road that had been fought over, and there were corpses of soldiers scattered on the asphalt. They aren't in the habit of burying the fallen here, and the approach to every combat zone can be recognized by the inhuman odor of decaying bodies. Some additional fermentation must take place in the putrid humidity of the tropics, because the smell is intense, terrible—so stunning that, no matter how many times I went to the front, I always felt dizzy and ready to vomit. We had jerrycans full of extra gasoline in the lead car, so we stopped and poured some on the corpses, and covered them with a few dry branches and roadside bushes; then the driver fired his automatic into the asphalt at such an angle that sparks flew and a fire started. We marked our route to Balombo with these fires.

Balombo is a little town in the forest that keeps changing hands. Neither side can settle in for good because of the forest, which allows the enemy to sneak to within point-blank range under cover and suddenly attack the town. This morning Balombo was taken by an MPLA detachment of a hundred people. There is still shooting in the surrounding woods because the enemy has retreated, but not very far. In Balombo, which is devastated, not a single civilian remains—only these hundred soldiers. There is water, and the girls from the detachment approach us freshly bathed, with their wet hair wound around curling papers. Carlotta admonishes them: They shouldn't behave as if preparing to go out for the evening; they ought to be ready to fight at all times. They complain that they had to attack in the first wave because the boys were not eager to advance. The boys strike their foreheads with their hands and say the girls are lying. They are all sixteen to eighteen years old, the age of our high school students or of the fighters in the Warsaw uprising. Part of the unit is joyriding up and down the main street on a captured tractor. Each group makes one circuit and hands the wheel over to the next one. Others have given up contending for the tractor and are riding around on captured bicycles. It is chilly in Balombo because it lies in the hills; there is a light breeze and the forest is rustling.

As the crew films, I walk along with them, snapping pictures. Carlotta, who is conscientious and doesn't let herself be carried away in the euphoria of victory sweeping the detachment, knows that a counterattack could begin at any time, or that snipers lurking under cover could be taking aim at our heads. So she accompanies us all the time with her automatic at the ready. She is attentive and taciturn. We can hear the tops of her boots rubbing together as she walks. Carvalho, the cameraman, films Carlotta walking against the background of burned-out houses, and later against a background of strikingly exuberant adenias. All of this will be shown in Portugal, in a country that Carlotta will never see. In another country, Poland, her pictures will also appear. We are still walking through Balombo and talking. Barbosa asks her when she will get married. Oh, she can't say—there's a war on. The sun sinks behind the trees; twilight is approaching and we must leave. We return to the cars, which are waiting on the main street. We're all satisfied because we have been to the front, we have film and pictures, we are alive. We get in as we did when we drove here: Carlotta in front, we in back. The driver starts the motor and puts the car in gear. And then—we all remember that it was exactly at that moment—Carlotta gets out of the car and says she is staying. "Carlotta," Alberto says, "come with us. We'll take you out to supper, and tomorrow we'll take you to Lisbon." Carlotta laughs, waves good-bye, and signals the driver to start.

We're sad.

We drive away from Balombo on a road that grows darker and darker, and we drive into the night. We arrive late in Benguela and locate the one restaurant still open; we want something to eat. Alberto, who knows everyone here, gets us a table in the open air. It's splendid—the air is cool and there's an ocean of stars in the sky. We sit down hungry and exhausted and talk. The food doesn't come for a long time. Alberto calls, but it's noisy and nobody hears us. Then lights appear at the corner and a car comes around and brakes sharply in front of the restaurant. A tired, unwashed soldier with a dirt-smeared face jumps out of the car. He says that immediately after our departure there was an attack on

Balombo and they have given up the town; in the same sentence, he says that Carlotta died in the attack.

We stood up from the table and walked into the deserted street. Each of us walked separately, alone; there was nothing to talk about. Hunched over, Alberto went first, with Carvalho behind him and Fernandez on the other side of the street, with Barbosa following and me at the end. It was better for us to reach the hotel that way and disappear from each other's sight. We had driven out of Balombo at a crazy speed and none of us had heard the shooting begin behind us. And so we hadn't been fleeing. But if we had heard the shots, would we have ordered the driver to turn back so we could be with Carlotta? Would we have risked our lives to protect her, as she had risked hers to protect us in Balombo? Maybe she had died covering us as we drove away, because the boys were chasing around on the tractor and the girls were doing their hair when the enemy appeared out of nowhere.

We are all culpable in Carlotta's death, since we agreed to let her stay behind; we could have ordered her to return. But who could have foreseen it? The most guilty are Alberto and I: We are the ones who wanted to go to the front, so Monti gave us an escort—that girl. But can we change anything now, call it off, run the day backward?

Carlotta is gone.

Who would have thought that we were seeing her in the last hour of her life? And that it was all in our hands? Why didn't Alberto stop the driver, get out, and tell her: Come with us because otherwise we'll stay and you'll be responsible! Why didn't any of us do that? And is the guilt any easier to bear because it is spread among the five of us?

Of course it was a tragic accident. That's how, lying, we will tell the story. We can also say there was an element of predestination, of fate, to it. There was no reason for her to stay there, and furthermore it had been agreed from the start that she would return with us. In the last second she was prompted by some indefinable instinct to get out of the car, and a moment later she was dead. Let's believe it was fate. In such situations we act in a way we can't explain afterward. And we say, Your Honor, I don't know how it happened, how it came to that, because in fact it began from nothing.

But Carlotta knew this war better than we did; she knew that dusk, the customary time for attack, was approaching, and that it would be better if she stayed there and organized cover for our departure. That must have been the reason for her decision. We thought of this later, when it was too late. But now can't ask her about anything.

We knock on the hotel door, which is already locked. The owner, a massive old black man, opens up and wants to hug us because we've made it back in one piece, he wants to ask us all about it. Then he looks at us carefully, falls silent, and walks away. Each of us takes his key, goes upstairs, and locks himself in his room.

Part IV

That small point disappearing into the sky is the plane in which Alberto and his crew are flying out. The throbbing of the motors rolls up over the airport, over the town, fainter and fainter but audible all the while as, for a long time after, the small, disappearing point floats away and then becomes invisible. It is as if the echoes of an unseen, distant storm among the stars were reaching us from space. Then it falls silent. The sky becomes immobile and fills with quiet and the morning glare. After a couple of hours, at the other end of the galaxy, a small point appears and begins to grow, to expand, until it assumes the stiff shape of a plane—which will mean that Alberto and his crew are landing in Europe.

And I fly out of Benguela, but in the other direction, to the south, where the African continent begins to come to an end and, after a thousand or more kilometers, beyond Namibia and the Kalahari, plunges into two oceans. When we arrived at the airport that morning, aside from Alberto's plane there was also a two-engine Friendship whose pilots—two unshaven, deadbeat Portuguese with red, sleepless eyes—said they were flying immediately to Lubango to pick up the last group of refugees there. Lubango, formerly Sá da Bandeira, lies 350 kilometers south of Benguela and is the headquarters of the southern front staff. I didn't have a pass to go there because no one is admitted to the southern front, the weakest, most neglected, worst organized, and most poorly armed front. But I thought I might get away with it. So I thought, although to tell the truth I wasn't thinking at all, because if I had really considered matters I might have lost the inclination to go. On the other hand, if I had considered the matter more carefully, I might have wanted to make the trip because, as I see it, it's wrong to write about people without living through at least a little of what they are living through. In any case, I began asking the pilots if they would take me along. They were so exhausted from unbroken stretches of flying, so indifferent to everything, that they didn't answer, which was probably a sign that they agreed. I was wearing jeans and a shirt, I had a pass for Benguela and a little money in my pocket, and I carried a camera. Everything else remained behind in the hotel, since there was neither time nor a car to get to town. Without waiting, therefore, I got into the empty plane and hid myself in a corner to avoid asserting my presence, just in case they thought better of it and ordered me to stay at the airport. A quarter of an hour later we took off from Benguela, flying first over the desert and then over the green hills, above a soft, enchanting piedmont landscape, and then over the great rainbow flower garden that is Lubango.

At the airport in Lubango a group of terrified, sweaty, apathetic Portuguese sat on kit bags and suitcases beside their even more terrified wives, and their children asleep in the women's arms. They rushed for the plane before it had even shut off its motors. I went up to a mulatto who was wandering around the apron and asked him if he could take me to staff headquarters. He said he would take me, but then immediately asked how I planned to get out, since this was the last plane leaving; it seemed to him that, although the town was in the hands of the MPLA, it was surrounded, and that the road to town was either in the hands of the enemy or could be by tomorrow. To this I gave no exact answer, aside from something like: As the Lord will have it.

Everything from that moment on happened as in an incomprehensible, incoherent dream in which unknown persons and unseen powers entangle us in a succession of situations from which there is no way out, and from which we awaken every now and then drenched in sweat, more and more exhausted and devoid of will. At the front staff headquarters (a residential quarter on a hill), I was greeted by a young white Angolan, a political commissar. His name was Nelson. He greeted me with joy, as if I were a guest he had been expecting all along—and sent me at once to a near-certain death.

Nelson had a restless, violent nature, mad ideas, and an impulsive, feverish manner. The first thing I told him was that I wanted to go to the front, and that was all it took for him to write out a pass for me. Before I could figure out what was going on he was pushing me outside, where a driver was just starting the motor of a big old Mercedes truck. I barely managed to beg Nelson to give me a cup of water, because I was ready to pass out from thirst. The truck was loaded to capacity with rifles, ammunition boxes, barrels of gasoline, and sacks of flour. On top of this cargo sat six soldiers. Nelson pushed me into the cab, where the driver was already seated—a half-naked black civilian, extraordinarily thin. A moment later Diogenes, the leader of the expedition, joined us in the cab, and we started off down the road immediately.

We drove through town—in those days every town in Angola looked like a ghastly, corroding movie set built on the outskirts of Hollywood and already abandoned by the film crew—and the green suddenly ended, the flowers disappeared, and we entered a hot, dry tropical flatland, overgrown as far as the eye could see with thick, thorny, leafless gray brush. A low gray gorge cut through this bush and at the bottom of the gorge ran the asphalt road. This was the road we were driving along in the truck. The Mercedes was so old and overloaded that no matter how the driver exerted himself, it would not do better than sixty kilometers an hour.

I was in a terrible situation, because I didn't know where we were going and couldn't bring myself to admit that I didn't. Diogenes might think, How come he doesn't know? What's he doing here, and why is he riding with us? He's riding with us and he doesn't know where we're going? Yet I really didn't know. I had accidentally come across the plane in Benguela and so found myself in Lubango. It was an accident that the mulatto I met at the airport took me to headquarters. A strange man about whom I knew nothing except that his name was Nelson, and whom I was seeing for the first time in my life, had put me in the truck. The truck had immediately driven off and now we were rolling between two walls of thorny bush toward a destination unknown to me. Everything had happened quickly and somehow so categorically that I could neither think about it nor say no.

So we drove along with the thin, anxious man cling-ing to the steering wheel at my left, me in the middle, and Diogenes on the right with his submachine gun pointed out the window, ready to fire. With the sun standing directly overhead, the cab was as hot as a fur-nace and reeked of oil and sweat. At a certain moment Diogenes, who had been looking steadily at the wall of bush on his side, asked, "Tell me, *camarada*, do you know where we're going?"

I replied that I didn't.

"And tell me, *camarada*," Diogenes went on without looking at me, "do you know what it means to drive down the road that we're on?"

Again I answered that I didn't.

Diogenes said nothing for a moment, because we were climbing a hill and the roar of the motor was deafening. Then he said, "*Camarada*, this road leads to South Af-rica. The border is four hundred fifty kilometers from here. The town of Pereira d'Eça is forty kilometers this side of the border. One of our units is there and that's where we're going. The cities, Lubango and Pereira d'Eça, are in our hands. But the enemy holds the coun-tryside. The enemy is in this bush that we're driving through, and this road belongs to him. None of our con-voys has got through to the unit in Pereira d'Eça for a month. All the trucks have been lost in ambushes. And now we're trying to get there. We have four hundred kilometers of road in front of us and at every meter we could fall into an ambush. Do you understand, *camarada*?"

I felt as if I couldn't produce any sound, so I merely nodded that I understood what it meant to drive down the road we were on. Later I got hold of myself enough to ask why there were so few of us. If a company or even a platoon were with us there would be a better chance of getting through. Diogenes answered that there were few people on this front in general. They had to be brought from Luanda and Benguela. The land here was almost uninhabited. There were a few nomads—wild people who walked around naked. They had lost all their wars many years ago. Since then they had known they couldn't win—their only hope was to hide in the bush. With a movement of his head, Diogenes indicated the wall of bush behind which these naked, defeated people were concealed. Next I asked why we were traveling in such a dilapidated truck. After all, the Portuguese had left so many splendid vehicles. Diogenes replied that the vehicles left by the Portuguese were the property of the Portuguese. There was no money to buy the trucks, and there wasn't even anybody to talk to, since the owners were in Europe. But wouldn't he agree, I pressed, that in a faster truck it would be easier to escape and harder to be hit, while by driving in a clunker like this we were rolling straight toward death? Yes, Diogenes agreed, but—he asked—what can we do? There was a gap in the conversation; the only sound was the roar of the motor and the whirr of the tires on the soft asphalt.

Time is passing, but we seem to be stuck in place. Constantly the same glimmering seam of asphalt laid on the loose red earth. Constantly the same faded, cracked wall of bush. The same blinding white sky. The same emptiness of a deserted world, an emptiness that betrays life neither by movement nor by voice. Our truck wobbles and rolls through this unmoving, dead landscape like a small tin car in the depths of a carnival shooting gallery. The owner turns the crank and the toy, stamped out of tin, bucks from side to side, and whoever wants to take a shot is welcome. In the back of the truck sit six soldiers hidden behind the ammunition boxes and sacks of flour. The sun is blazing mercilessly, so they pull the tarpaulin over themselves as if driving through a downpour. They are better off because, if we drive into an ambush, they can jump out of the truck and flee into the bush. The predicament of those in the cab is worse. Trapped in the metal box, they are like three moving targets tilting slowly forward and perfectly illuminated by the sun at the sixteenth parallel. The little tin car moves in the banal interior of the empty shooting gallery and the owner notes, with growing astonishment, that nobody wants to shoot at it. After all, it costs little to win an attractive prize. He turns the crank more and more drowsily and perfunctorily. The tin cutout moves slower, slower, until it comes to a halt.

We pull off to the side of the road. Ahead of us, on the same side, lies the wreck of a burned-out truck—the remains of a convoy that made it this far. Scattered cans, barrels, sacks, tires. In one place, scorched earth and charred bones. Whoever caught them must have killed them and then burned them, or even tied them up and burned them alive. It's impossible to say who survived, or whether anyone survived at all. Diogenes says that if anyone escaped into the bush, they couldn't have gone far; they would have died of thirst because there is no water here. They could survive only on the road, but on the road they could be killed. You have to keep to the road, but of course you can be ambushed. All right, there is no better way out, which means there is no perfect way out. That is what Diogenes says, and he observes that those who died in this burned-out truck must have made a mistake, they must have been traveling in the early morning or at dusk or at night. Then it's cool and the enemy has the strength to come out onto the road and spring an ambush. At noon, on the other hand, the heat is going full blast and a deathly sleepiness and indolence seize the combatants. They retreat into the shade and drift into slumber. Martial enthusiasm sputters out and enmity grows tepid. You have to take advantage of this and travel at high noon, the safest time. I remember that Monti said the same thing. The front falls asleep when the sun stands at its zenith.

We drove until dusk under pressure, in an intent, helpless alertness, passing two more charred trucks from lost convoys. Diogenes urged the driver on, forbidding him to halt. At five in the afternoon we saw several armed people standing in the road. They stood there, pointing their automatic rifles toward us. Diogenes took his Kalashnikov off the safety and the soldiers in back got up from where they had been lying and, taking cover behind the cab, took aim at the people in the road. The driver slowed down and the distance between the truck and the people ahead decreased. Nobody fired. Then, when we were close—close enough to make out their figures and even their faces—one of the people in the road pointed his rifle upward and fired a round. Diogenes pulled his pistol out of his holster and also shot into the air. The Mercedes stopped and the people in the road came running up.

"Commandante Farrusco's unit," one of them said.

"Commandante Diogenes's convoy," Diogenes answered.

We were in Pereira de'Eça. They asked for cigarettes.

I reached into my pocket and only then, when everything in me broke and subsided into loose, relaxed, calm particles, did I notice that my trousers and shirt were drenched in sweat, that I was wet all over, and that in my pocket, where there had been a pack of Polish Radomskie Extra-Strongs, I had nothing but a handful of damp hay smelling of nicotine.

The wrecked billboard on the way into town offers a chance to rest your eyes: "In Pereira d'Eça," it says, "Stop at the Black Swan Inn. Air-Conditioning—Home Cooking—Garden—Bar—Attractive Prices." And a clumsy drawing of a bird swimming in a lake that at this latitude could appear only in a dream. This is an inducement to those who have been around the world and grown acquainted with distant continents and unfamiliar territories. The traveler along the sterile and monotonous road from Luanda to Windhoek—2230 kilometers—can find a comfortable stopping place here. May I impart a word of advice to the weary wayfarer? Don't stop in this town tonight. Not these days. Times have changed and the promised comfort is lacking. There may be water, indeed, but there are no lights. It's dark. The moon doesn't rise. There are only stars, but somehow distant ones, faint and not very helpful. It's not a good place to sleep, because the houses have been smashed and looted. Nor is the cuisine to be recommended. On the concrete floor of the inn, in a puddle of dried blood, lies a butchered goat that has already begun to reek. Anyone who's hungry carves out a hunk of meat with a bayonet and roasts it over the bonfire. How do these people live? Why don't they die of poisoning from carrion virus? Nor can one count on the advertised air-conditioning. It is sweltering and not even at night does the heat lift from the earth; it crushes the languidly, viscously unmoving, flattened town.

In the glare of an oil lamp, the only light, three faces are visible, covered with sweat, shining as if smeared with olive oil. The wide, bearded face of Commandante Farrusco. The pale face, covered with adolescent pimples, of his assistant Carlos, the hero of Luso. The prematurely destroyed, uncared-for face of a woman named Esperança. We are sitting in the inn on crates and stools, but the leader has settled in an armchair. Outside the window soldiers drift around the plaza, dissolving into the gloom, black, like darkness set in motion. "Why aren't they going to their posts?" Farrusco asks, but he falls silent and gives no orders. The rest remain quiet; it was evidently a meaningless question, although the answer is known. It is obvious that going to their posts wouldn't improve anything, wouldn't help. This is a unit sentenced to annihilation; there is no saving it.

"Bring in the one who came from the south," Farrusco orders the people standing in the doorway, or rather in the place where there had once been a door leading to the wooden veranda and the square. "Listen to what this man says, *camarada*," Farrusco tells me, because it turns out they have already talked to him in the afternoon and know what he has to say. In walks an extremely tired, jittery Portuguese. He has sunken eyes, he is unshaven and dirty, and looks like the personification of helplessness and abandonment. His name is Humberto Dos Angos de Freitas Quental. He is from here, he was born here—about fifty years ago, I would guess. A week ago he escaped to Namibia with his family. He left his wife and four children in a camp for Portuguese at Windhoek and decided to return himself. He wanted to return because his mother had stayed in Pereira d'Eça. His mother is eighty-one and has been running a bakery for as long as her son Humberto, who is standing here, has been alive. She told her son that she was not leaving and that she was going to keep on baking bread, which is always needed. "And you yourselves know," Humberto tells us, "that in Pereira d'Eça you have fresh bread." Yes, the whole unit knows that, living as they do on the bread baked by that woman and furthermore not paying for it, because this is a volunteer liberation army without money. When he left to take his family to Namibia, the supplies of flour were running out and his mother—who is deaf and doesn't understand that there is a war on, and who for reasons of age no longer understands anything, except that as long as the world exists people will need bread—ordered her son to return with flour. She stayed there alone, so he decided to come back and bring her the flour, which was confiscated on the border, but he knows that a truck carrying flour has arrived today from Lubango, which means that his mother will again be baking bread and there will again be something free to eat, because she doesn't ask for money.

"We all love that woman," Farrusco says, "even though she isn't exactly for us, but she's for life and bread, and that's enough. Our people brought her the water that she needed. And they brought her wood. And she's going to live just as long as we live, or maybe even longer. But I want you to tell these people who've come from Lubango what you heard in Windhoek and what they told you along the road in that place, what do you call it?"

"It's called Tsumeb," said the son of the baker, "and it's perhaps two hundred fifty kilometers from here. The Portuguese who fled there said that before long the South African army would advance into Angola and chase out the MPLA. They said the same thing in Windhoek. They said the army would move today, perhaps tomorrow. They have armor and an air force and they'll occupy Luanda."

"How do you know?" asked Farrusco.

"That's what all the Portuguese say," Humberto replied, "even though it's a secret. In Windhoek, South African army officers came to our camp and asked who had served in the army, and if anybody wanted to join the forces that were going to strike Angola. And in Tsumeb, at the gas station, one white told me that the town was full of armored vehicles that would advance into Angola tomorrow or the next day to finish off the communists."

Farrusco told the baker's son he could go home. Humberto had made an honest impression. But he didn't seem too bright and was probably illiterate. We stayed alone in the room; it was still hot and close, even though it was past midnight. Some people were sleeping on the floor, propped against the wall, while others were coming and going for no known reason, without saying a word. "Check whether they've gone to their posts," Farrusco told Carlos. "Send a few along the road toward the border. Let them go some distance and see what's happening."

"What good will it do?" says Esperança. Her face was now darker than it had been in the evening.

"Tell them to really go," Farrusco says, "and not to be afraid and not to hide in the ditch."

"If they go too far," the woman insists, "they could be cut off or ambushed. The enemy's all around."

"All right," says Farrusco, "but I want to know exactly where they are."

"Well, those patrols aren't going to find out," says Esperança, "because they're going to die. Why do you want to stir up the army? We don't have the strength to defend ourselves."

Commandante Farrusco's unit numbers 120. It is the only unit on the southern front between Lubango and the border (450 kilometers) and between the Atlantic and Zambia (1200 kilometers). The only unit in a region one-third the size of Poland. All around, for scores, for hundreds of kilometers, stretches the barren bush, without water, without reference points—an unappeased wilderness of millions of barbed branches woven into walls, a hostile world not to be conquered, not to be penetrated. There is only the road to Lubango, the one route through it, like a corridor lined with barbed wire along which retreat is impossible because it is too far to go on foot and there is too little transport to carry the whole unit. It's possible that at this hour, nearly two in the morning, the enemy has seized the road on both sides of the town and we are sitting here in the shadow of a steel-jaw trap waiting for somebody to trip the spring, at which point there will be a deafening snap.

Diogenes and one other man from the convoy came in, and then Carlos returned. The leader asked if they had gone out on patrol and Carlos said yes. He sat on a crate and unbuckled his belt, to which he had clipped a whole arsenal of pistols, cartridges, and grenades. In colonial times Carlos and Farrusco had fought in Portuguese commando units. Both were farmer's sons from southern Portugal. After their army tours they stayed in Angola and worked as auto mechanics.

Later Nelson told me what happened next: "When the MPLA uprising against FNLA and UNITA broke out that summer, there was also fighting in Lubango. But a lot of whites were fighting in the enemy ranks. In our region, in the south, the fate of the uprising hung in the balance a long time. One day a stocky, bearded man walked into headquarters and said, 'I'll show you how to do it—how to fight.' That was Farrusco. He organized a unit, took Lubango, and later captured Pereira d'Eça and stayed there. He lacked arms. The whole time they had only their rifles and two 82-millimeter mortars. Farrusco and Carlos fired the mortars. They held them in their hands, without using the base, so both had burned palms from the hot barrels. Their hands were all blisters and sores."

Everyone is vigilant at the inn tonight—a dull, unarmed, expectant vigilance. The only ones asleep may well be the boys at the outposts on the edge of town and in the ditches, because the sleep of the young is stronger than fear, thirst, or even mosquitoes. The oil lamp is burning in the room; silence. Nobody wants to talk or even knows what to talk about. Everybody is waiting for the dawn, growing more enervated and sleepy. There is a sound of snoring from those asleep on the floor, and the dirge of the mosquitoes. Sweat trickles down your face and your mouth is bitter from nicotine, dry and nauseating.

I nudged Farrusco's shoulder because he was starting to nod. I wanted to return to Lubango today and then push on to Luanda. I thought that what the Portuguese said was important. He struck me as truthful. "Sure, it's important," Farrusco agreed. "They're starting their invasion."

"From here to Luanda," I told him, "is fifteen hundred kilometers. I don't know when I'll get there because there are no more planes. In Luanda I can get in touch with Poland, and I think that what the Portuguese said is world news. Do something so I can get back to Lubango today."

"We have to wait for dawn because you can't use that road at night," Farrusco said. "The lights are visible too far off and you can easily be ambushed. We'll see what happens at dawn; we'll see whether they attack. Between the border and Pereira d'Eça we have nobody. They could also move from the dam at Ruacana and cut our road to Lubango. From here there's no other way to go, only along that road, which may already have been cut in the night because their army is stationed in Ruacana and from there a three-hour ride brings them to our road."

The night ended and a red glow rose above the earth. Houses and trees appeared, and at the edge of town stood the wall of bush. The scouts returned and reported that they had encountered no one on the road. The tension eased slightly. Farrusco left to check the outposts. I moved along behind him. Where the sandy streets stopped at the edge of the forest, soldiers lay waiting to see if anything was moving among the trees. The bush resounded with splendid avian music; a noisy tropical hosanna was floating upward. Then the sun came up, the beams broke through as if a spotlight had come on, and everything suddenly quieted down.

We returned to the inn. The woman was making coffee and it smelled like dawn at a campground in Masuria. Only now did I notice the staff map on the wall. A tack in the middle of it represented the unit at Pereira d'Eça. There were no other tacks anywhere around it. Only higher up—a tack in Lubango, a tack in Moçâmedes, another in Matala. The higher up, the more tacks. A thick black diagonal line, slightly broken into steps, was our road. At the bottom, a row of crosses on the bank of the Cunene River was the border with Namibia. An arrow at the top showed the direction to Europe. The areas covered with little circles were bush. The areas covered with dots . . . desert. The blue area . . . the Atlantic. PN . . . a park—lions, elephants, antelope. 5 in red: five of ours dead. 7 in black: seven of theirs dead. More red and black digits in two columns at the bottom, without a line for the totals, because death's account is always open.

Now, God help us, to drive along the thick black line, upward to Lubango—alive. We set out under a high sun at ten, hoping that the maddening heat would force the enemy out of his ambushes and drive him into a state of helpless somnolence. Soldiers befuddled by the heat drifted around the scorching plaza, wandering in circles apathetically. Others sat in the shade, leaning against the walls of houses, against fences, against trees, as immobile as victims of African sleeping sickness. I don't know what happened to Diogenes; he and the whole crew of the convoy had disappeared. I didn't see the woman anywhere. Carlos stood on the veranda of the inn and waved his automatic in our direction. In the immobile scenery of this plaza, Carlos's arm swiveling in the air seemed to be the one thing alive and capable of movement.

We rode in a Toyota jeep driven by Antonio, a sixteen-year-old soldier. A dazzling brilliance, a lake of pulsing light that moved forward, settled above the pavement. At a certain moment a vehicle emerged from the depths of this lake, like a phantom. It drew nearer to us. You never know who is coming from the opposite direction and Farrusco, sitting at my right, took the safety off his Ka-2 and unhooked a grenade from his belt. The vehicles stopped. An unkempt, unshaven Portuguese stepped out of a pickup truck loaded like a gypsy wagon with bedding; he was fleeing to South Africa with his whole family. He stood on the road hunched over and resigned, as if facing a judge who would sentence him, any moment now, to life imprisonment. He said that the road was empty and nobody had stopped him. But that meant nothing because the people who set ambushes usually didn't bother refugees.

It was an open jeep and the rush of air provided some relief. It whistled in our ears. "This year," Farrusco shouted to me through the wind, "I've had a son born to me. He's in Lubango and I want to see him."

"Is he big?" I asked as loud as I could, so he would hear me.

"Big," he beamed. "A big boy." We passed Roçadas and then the deserted bridge over the Cunene. "My father didn't have any land and there were eight of us," the commander shouted through the wind. "All without shoes. I don't know if you're aware that we have mountains and it's cold up there."

I shook my head: I hadn't known. The jeep was traveling along the road through a landscape so monotonous that we seemed to be standing still. "When I was fighting as a commando," I heard him say through the wind, "it struck me that I was on the wrong side. That's why," he added after a moment, coughing because the wind had dried out his throat, "when this war started I went over to the other side."

We had arrived at the worst place, Humbe. Here the road along which the South African units might have advanced ran off to Ruacana. Farrusco ordered the vehicle to halt. He walked along the edge of the bush toward the crossroads to assess the situation. He noticed nothing suspicious and encountered nobody. "Putting one armored vehicle there," he said, "would be enough to paralyze the whole road. We could do nothing because we have no antitank weapons.

"In Europe," he said, "they taught me that a front is trenches and barbed wire, which form a distinct and visible line. A front on a river, along a road, or from village to village. You can trace it on a map with a pencil or point to it on the terrain. But here the front is everywhere and nowhere. There is too much land and too few people for a front line to exist. This is a wild, unorganized world and it's hard to come to terms with it. There is no water, because there is a lot of desert here. You can't hold out for long where there are no springs, and it's a long way between springs. Here where we're standing, there is water, but the next water is a hundred kilometers away. Every unit holds on to its water, because otherwise it dies. If there are a hundred kilometers between water, that space is nobody's and there's nobody there. So the front doesn't consist of a line here, but of points, and moving points at that. There are hundreds of fronts because there are hundreds of units. Every unit is a front, a potential front. If our unit runs into an enemy unit, those two potential fronts turn into real fronts. A battle occurs. We are a three-man potential front now, traveling northward. If we are ambushed, we become a real front. This is a war of ambushes. On any road, at any place, there can be a front. You can travel the whole country and come back alive, or you can die a meter from where you're standing. There are no principles, no methods. Everything comes down to luck and happenstance. This war is a real mess. Nobody knows just where they stand."

At exactly noon we were going full speed, lashed by the sultry wind. The bush rushed backward and disappeared behind us. We passed Cahama and Chibemba; burned houses stood by the road. "If you make it to Luanda," Farrusco shouted through the blast of wind, "say that they should send people and arms. Say that if they move in from Namibia, we won't be able to hold this ground." We rode a long time in silence. Later I heard his voice again. "I think they are going to kill me," he screamed over the wind. "I think they will spot the white commander driving this road and they will kill me. It's very hard," he shouted, "very hard to get out of an ambush, because it's always too late, you walk right into their sights, but you know," he cried, "I'm not afraid, listen, I don't feel any fear!"

I heard a crash, a bang, hammering, a voice—"Let's go, let's go!" It was the voice of the restless spirit, Commissar Nelson. I got up. It was dark all around and fortunately I was sleeping in my clothes and shoes, so I could run right after him and we flew down the stairs and my head hurt. Only in the car did I start to come round. It was a new Peugeot 504, gray. Nelson was driving. Beside him sat Commandante Bota from front headquarters, drunk. He was holding a bottle of whisky between his knees. In the back with me sat Nelson's friend and aide Manuel. Manuel had an Uzi machine pistol, an Israeli weapon handy at close quarters but of little use in ambushes, where the greater range of the Soviet Ka-2 or Belgian G-3 makes them better to fight with. I looked at my watch; it was two in the morning. Lubango lies high above sea level and the nights here are icy, Scandinavian. I trembled from cold and sleeplessness. "Where are we going?" I asked Manuel. "To Benguela." I cheered up and was trying to get back to sleep when Manuel said there was a battle ahead. I woke up at once. "Chipenda's force is attacking," Manuel said, "and ahead of us is only our one unit led by Commandante Antonio, but Antonio is in Benguela, where he went to look for weapons."

"So why are we traveling along a road where there's a battle?" I asked Manuel.

"Because there's no other road from Lubango to Benguela," he replied.

"Well, you've got a point there," I admitted.

Bota took a pull from his bottle and then passed it back to us, so we all got a swig. Things improved. We rode for perhaps half an hour at high speed through hilly terrain with green forests on both sides of us and we had already reached the crossing in Caculi when we heard shooting, the drawn-out thumping of machine guns and the bursting of shells to left and right just off the road. Nelson turned off the lights and slowed down, because the night was very dark; he drove on blind, feeling for the soft shoulder of the road. "Slower," commanded Bota, who was beginning to sober up. "But perhaps it's better to go faster," Manuel said shyly. We drove on like that for centuries. Jesus, I thought, Jesus, a grenade has gone off in the ditch—there was a banging of tin as if someone were hammering on the roof with a club. After a moment Bota asked, "Is everybody okay?" "Yes, we're okay." Then, at the last instant, Nelson saw a parked truck and was about to swerve around it, when a mulatto jumped out of the ditch toward him and said, "Nelson, I've got twenty people here, but I can't throw them forward to hold Chipenda, because I'm out of gasoline. Where can I get gasoline?" He was all shivers and it was terribly cold.

"Where will I get you gasoline?" Nelson said. "Go to Lubango."

"How can I go to Lubango, man, when I don't have any way to move?"

A series of tracers ripped above us and then a second and a third, and the man who was standing in the road and gripping the door of the car as if he didn't want to let us go, said, "Nelson, I'm telling you, it's bad, they're killing us off like chickens." Again a grenade nearby, then several at once, and Bota said "Move on" from the bottom of his soused stupefaction. Nelson put it in gear and the mulatto disappeared as suddenly as if he had been struck down, and why were we driving into that horrendous fire instead of sitting it out in the ditch? But they might have thought that the enemy would round us up like stray dogs and that it would be better to try to slip out of the trap, and in any case we turned at Quilengues and along both sides there were walls of earth and we were obviously diving into the bottom of some excavation or gorge, and suddenly running feet and two boys ran out with rifles and Bota said, "Stop them!" and Nelson cried "Halt!" and they stopped. They were just kids, beat-up and half-paralyzed with fear, and I looked at their rifles—they had old Mausers. "Where are you from?" Bota asked. "From Commandante Antonio's regiment." "Aha," Bota says, "you're running away, eh?" They stood there, humble, frightened, as if teacher had caught them copying during a quiz. Bota ordered, "Return to the battle immediately, and I'll be there right away to see if you're fighting, and I'll remember your faces." Gray with fear, the faces of these boys withdrew into the darkness and vanished. We drove on and Bota said, "Now it'll be worse still, because what we're trying to do is push through to Quilengues and there ought to be mercenaries there."

Dawn begins and the shooting slowly quiets down and we leave it behind. The sky begins to resemble a meadow and then it looks like a sea and then like a snow-covered plain. "Halt!" says Bota, and Nelson stops the Peugeot on a blind curve. We walk ahead to see what is going on in Quilengues. It is a cold, gray dawn; dew, no sun. We advance on the prowl because no one can tell who is hiding in these houses and who's around the next streetcorner or the one after that. We walk for a long time to convince ourselves that the town is empty, without a trace of life. I don't know what happened there before we arrived. There are no people. Nor any other creatures. Not a dog, not a cat. No goats and no chickens. No birds in the trees. Perhaps not even mice.

We had returned calmer to the car when Nelson suddenly stopped, straightened his shoulders, and said, "Another day of life," because now the road to Benguela was clear, and he began to do calisthenics and we all joined in, Bota unsteadily, staggering continually, leaning to left and right, but we were doing it energetically. Put your hands on your hips, now stand on tiptoe and do a squat, and one and two, straighten your backs, head up, deeper squats, deeper, and now thrust your arms forward and back, harder, harder to the back and exhale, inhale, arms out, don't let those arms droop, now lean forward and to the side on a three count and one and two and three and now a duck waddle and now jumping jacks and now the sun comes out.

Part V

When I returned to Luanda on Saturday morning it was still dark. We had ridden from Benguela in a tanker truck sent at night to the capital to look for gasoline, because the southern front was immobilized by lack of fuel. Along the way we passed drowsy, half-conscious checkpoints and boys wrapped in tarpaulins, in horse blankets, in bedspreads and sacks, since it was drizzling unpleasantly. As usual, discussions broke out among them over whether or not to let us pass, and they wanted us to give them something to eat or smoke, but we had nothing so they waved their hands in resignation and went back to sleep. You could have driven in at night and taken Luanda without a shot. Women in the African suburbs were lighting fires in front of their houses and preparing to grind manioc. Grinding manioc into a hard, crunchy white dough consumes half the lives of African women. The other half is earmarked for carrying and giving birth to children. In some places there were already lines waiting for water at the wells; in others, for bread. The people in these lines snoozed against walls or slept, covered with sheets, on the ground. Glued to the walls were posters reading YOUR COUNTRY NEEDS YOU with a giant black finger pointing at the eyes of passersby, which at that hour were clotted with sleep. In the European city center there was not a sign of life. Dust and cobwebs had overgrown the houses and streets.

I returned to room 47 in the hotel, drove a herd of cockroaches out of the bed, and lay down to sleep. I never dream, but this time I suddenly found myself in the woods outside Warsaw, where hooligans with knives were ducking in and out from behind the bushes, drawing nearer, as if playing hide-and-seek. I opened my eyes to see Dona Cartagina, the thin and exhausted Oscar (now owner of the hotel), and the doorman Fernando—with a plastic medallion bearing the likeness of Agostinho Neto around his neck—standing over me. They were happy that I had returned and, quite pointlessly, kept asking me if I was alive—with such insistence and incredulity that in the end I couldn't tell if I was awake, or if this was still a dream in which Cartagina, Oscar, and Fernando were suddenly prowling with knives through a grove of trees outside Warsaw. I don't know what happened next (I probably went back to sleep), because when I got out of bed the room was empty. There was a musty dampness in the air, and the ceiling fan was out of order. I tried turning the faucet. The faucet snorted violently, then silence: no water. I ran downstairs, where Felix was dozing at the reception desk with his elbows folded on heaps of unneeded paper and a stack of valueless money, his pale face reposing motionless and expressionless in his hands. I shook him: "Give me something to drink, Felix!" He opened his eyes and looked at me. "There's been no water for three days," he said. "The last wells are running dry. When there's nothing to drink, the city will have to give up." I left him and headed for the kitchen, but when I opened the door such a macabre odor assailed my nostrils that my legs grew heavy and I couldn't take a step. The stench emanated from a mountain of unwashed dishes and pots, but above all from a fetid pig that the black cook was quartering with a cleaver. "*Camarada*," I said, leaning on the table to keep from dropping over, "give me water." He put down the cleaver and gave me a mug of water from a tin barrel. I felt a softness and a chill inside me: I was coming back to life. "Give me some more," I said. He consented: "Drink as much as it takes for you to feel good, *camarada*."

I locked myself in my room to make a phone call. The telephone worked. The concept of totality exists in theory, but never in life. In even the best-built wall there is always a chink (or we hope there is, and that means something). Even when we have the feeling that nothing works anymore, something works and makes a minimal existence possible. Even if there's an ocean of evil around us, green and fertile islets will poke above the water. They can be seen, they are on the horizon. Even the worst situation in which we can find ourselves breaks down into elements that include something for us to grab hold of, like the branch of a bush that grows on the bank, to avoid being sucked to the bottom by the whirlpool. That chink, that island, that branch sustain us on the surface of existence.

Thus in our closed city, where thousands of things had ceased functioning, just when it seemed that everything was ruined, the telephone nevertheless worked. From the south, from the border with Namibia, I had brought news that today or perhaps tomorrow the armored columns would roll into Angola. The baker's son had reported that the South African army was already in Tsumeb, ready for war. They would need three hours to drive to the border, three days to drive to Benguela, and perhaps another week to drive to Luanda. No one in Luanda knew this, because the capital had no contact with the rest of the country. I wanted to pass along what the baker's son and Farrusco had said: that the intervention had been set in motion and that the southern front wouldn't hold. I started phoning around, but none of the numbers answered. I tried again and again. The signal droned on and nobody anywhere picked up the telephone. I looked at the calendar, because I no longer had a feeling for time, which means that time had lost all sense of division for me, all measurability, it had fallen apart, it had oozed out like a dense tropical exhalation. Concrete time had ceased to signify anything and for a long while now the fact that it was Wednesday or Friday, the tenth or the twentieth, eight in the morning or two in the afternoon, had meant nothing to me. Life had propelled me from event to event in an undefined process directed toward an unseen goal. I knew only that I wanted to be here until the end, regardless of when it came, or how. Everything was a total puzzle that absorbed and fascinated me.

Using the calendar, I calculated that it was October 18, 1975. And, as I now remembered, Saturday. That explained the silence of the telephones. Because on Saturday and Sunday all life died away. Those two days were governed by their own inviolable laws. The guns fell silent and the war was suspended. People put down their weapons and fell asleep. Sentries left their posts and observers put away their binoculars. The roads and the streets emptied. Headquarters and offices were closed. Markets were depopulated. Radio stations went off the air. Buses stopped running. In an incomprehensible but absolute way, this vast country with its war and destruction, its aggression and poverty, came to a halt, went motionless as if someone had cast a spell, as if it were enchanted. Neither the most titanic explosion nor any heavenly apparition nor any human appeal could budge it from its weekend lethargy. Worst of all, I could never establish what happened to the people. The closest friends disappeared like stones in water. They were not at home and not in the streets. Yet they couldn't have traveled outside the city. Clubs, restaurants, and cafés—they didn't exist. I don't know—I can't explain it.

All the warring sides respected this weekend rest, and the bitterest enemies acknowledged the opponent's right to two days of relaxation. In this matter there were no divisions; the weekend laxity swept up and united everyone. These people were constructed in such a way that their vital energy lasted from Monday to Friday, after which they passed at midnight into a state of nirvana, into nonexistence, freezing in the positions they were in at that hour. Everything was enveloped in an apathetic silence that had the effect of a sleeping potion. Even nature seemed to go to sleep. The wind died down, the palms stiffened, and the fauna disappeared into the earth.

Oscar came in the evening with a telephone number written on a piece of paper, saying that I was to call it. "Whose number is it?" I asked. He didn't know. They had phoned the hotel and said to give me that number when I returned to Luanda. Oscar left me alone in the room. I picked up the receiver and dialed the number written on the paper. At the other end of the line, a low masculine voice answered. I said they had given me that number in the hotel and said to call. Was I named such-and-such? asked the low voice. Of course, I said. The first part of the conversation had been in Portuguese, but at that moment the other switched to Spanish and from his way of speaking and his accent I realized that I was speaking to a Cuban. Anyone who has spent some time in Latin America and knows Spanish can immediately distinguish the Cuban accent: It has a specific melody and is a slaphappy fusion of words whose endings are regularly omitted. I asked the other who he was and what he was doing, thinking that he was a reporter from *Prensa Latina* or someone of that order. Then he said, "Man, don't ask too much because whoever asks too much gets too much of an answer." I shut up, since I didn't know what he was talking about. "We'll see you in your room," he said. "We'll be there in an hour." And he hung up.

Two of them came, in civilian clothes, and one was black and massive and robust, and the other was white and stocky and short. They sat down and the black one took out a pack of Populares, a brand of Cuban cigarettes that I like. They asked if I had ever been in Cuba.

"Yes, I was there once."

"But where?"

"I was everywhere, in Oriente, in Camagüey, in Matanzas."

The black is from Oriente. "It's beautiful there, right?" he laughs.

"Beautiful," I say. "They took me up a magnificent mountain. The view was fantastic."

"Have you been south of here lately?" the white asked.

"Yes, I have."

"What's it like down there?"

"What's it like? First tell me who you are."

The white said, "We're from the army. From a group of instructors."

This was something new to me—I didn't know there were Cuban instructors in Angola. In Benguela I had seen a few people in Cuban uniforms, but they wear every conceivable kind of uniform here, whatever they get from abroad or on the front, so I thought they were MPLA soldiers. Now I asked, "Were those guys I saw in Benguela yours?"

"Yes," said the black, "ours. We've got a dozen or so people there."

I said maybe they had come too late, since by my calculations the South African army might already be deep inside Angola. Anyway, what could a dozen or so people do? They were facing a strong regular army. The South Africans had a lot of armor and artillery. They were Afrikaners and Afrikaners know how to fight. And the MPLA had no weapons. I said that Farrusco's unit had only two mortars and a few old rifles. There were no heavy weapons in Lubango, either. The one armored vehicle that used to be in Benguela had been taken out by the mercenaries. Who could put up any resistance to the armored columns that were coming, or might already have come, from Namibia? Besides, the past weighed heavily on the fate of the war. In this country the black man had lost every war with the white man for five hundred years. You couldn't change the way people think overnight. The MPLA soldier could whip the FNLA or UNITA soldier, but he would fear the white army coming from the south.

They agreed that the situation was difficult. We fell silent. It was dark from smoke in the room, and humid. We sat there sweating, tormented by thirst. I was fighting against my imagination because the vision of a bottle of beer or chilled juice with ice or some similar madness kept appearing before my eyes. I asked them if more aid was coming. They didn't know. It might come, but when and how, nobody could say. They had just arrived and were supposed to train this army, but it wasn't an army in our understanding of the term. There were loose units scattered around the country. Would there be time to make an army out of them? The enemy was twenty kilometers from Luanda. Mobutu was sending more and more battalions. They might march in tomorrow.

I led them downstairs. They said that we would have our next meeting at their place, because it was awkward for them to come to the hotel where various people were hanging around. They would send a car for me when the time came. I asked what I was to call them. I was to call the black one Mauricio and the white one Pablo. But if I telephoned it would be better not to use any names; instead, say in Spanish that a friend wanted to meet them. They would see to the rest. In a dark side street stood a covered jeep, new, with no license plates. The hand of someone sitting inside opened the door. They got in and the jeep drove away.

But there at staff headquarters in Pretoria and later in Windhoek and finally (a small detail) at the front headquarters in Tsumeb, everything was precisely and capably thought out. Maps on the walls: Africa in miniature but still large, from floor to ceiling and from the entrance all along the commander's wall, with the uninhabited regions marked in a sandy color. The higher-ranking staff officers at the long tables: experts who know it all inside out.

The name of the operation: Orange.

The goal of the operation: to occupy Luanda by November 10, 1975 (at 1800 hours on that day, in accordance with the Alvor agreement, the last Portuguese units were to leave Angola). The next day, announce the independence of Angola, with power passing into the hands of an FNLA-UNITA coalition government.

Coordination: a strike from the south along the Tsumeb–Pereira d'Eça–Lubango–Benguela–Novo Redondo–Luanda road. A simultaneous strike from the north along the Maquela do Zombo–Carmona–Caxito–Luanda road. A simultaneous strike from the east along the Nova Lisboa–Quibala–Dondo–Luanda road.

Forces, southern flank: motorized units of the South African army (support: units of Portuguese volunteers, FNLA and UNITA units, the Chipenda force). Northern flank: FNLA units (support: units of the Republic of Zaïre army, units of Portuguese volunteers). Eastern flank: same as for the northern flank.

Zero hour:—

(Here begins a discussion in English-Afrikaans-Portuguese. Two opinions collide. One faction favors beginning the action earlier, because the enemy might put up resistance; breaking down resistance takes time and could delay the occupation of Luanda. Besides, to the degree that moving into Angola will extend the army's supply lines for ammunition, fuel, and food, it is necessary to allow additional time. They propose Monday, October 20, for zero hour. Others contend that the operation will not take more than two weeks. In the north we are already in the suburbs of Luanda. All information indicates that the enemy will not be able to mount any resistance in the south. We'll move quickly in Panhard armored vehicles. It is enough to calculate the driving time of these vehicles from Tsumeb to Luanda and then factor in time for the units to have meals and sleep. They contend that a zero hour of October 27 will be sufficient. The first, more cautious variant finally prevails. Even if it takes three weeks, it will be a blitzkrieg to dazzle the world.)

Zero hour: Sunday, October 19.

On Sundays, as I mentioned, the country is immersed in a state of nonexistence and manifests no signs of life. Today, however, informed by an incomprehensible presentiment, Commandante Farrusco has been hunting his driver Antonio since morning and in the end Antonio has appeared on his own, sleepy and unconscious with exhaustion. Farrusco orders him to get behind the wheel and in the same red Toyota jeep that I returned from Pereira d'Eça in, they drive along the road through the bush. A while later they spot something in the rays of the sun that could almost be a phantom but quickly materializes and assumes the shape of a drawn-out column of armored vehicles above which hovers a bulging, nearly motionless helicopter. Another moment and the nervous rattling of machine guns rings out. Farrusco is badly wounded, shot through the lungs. Antonio is hit in the leg but remains conscious. He backs up and rushes in the opposite direction with his severely wounded commander.

The column moves forward toward Pereira d'Eça. The soldiers ride hidden inside the vehicles, but it must be hot and stuffy for them because—contrary to orders—here and there, in more and more of the armored personnel carriers, the hatch opens and a young, tanned face appears.

And in Luanda? What can you do on Sunday in our abandoned city, upon which—as it turns out—sentence has already been passed? You can sleep until noon.

You can turn on the faucet to check—ha!—just in case there is water.

You can stand before the mirror, thinking: so many gray hairs in my beard already.

You can sit in front of a plate on which lies a piece of disgusting fish and a spoonful of cold rice.

You can walk, sweating from weakness and effort, up the Rua de Luis de Camões, toward the airport or down toward the bay.

And yet that's not all—you can go to the movies, too! That's right, because we still have a movie theater, only one in fact, but it is panoramic and in the open air and, to top it off, free. The theater lies in the northern part of town, near the front. The owner fled to Lisbon but the projectionist remained behind, and so did a print of the famous porno film *Emmanuelle*. The projectionist shows it uninterrupted, over and over, gratis, free for everyone, and crowds of kids rush in, and soldiers who have got away from the front, and there's always a full house, a crush, and an uproar and indescribable bellowing. To enhance the effect, the projectionist stops the action at the hottest moments. The girl is naked—stop. He has her in the airplane—stop. She has her by the river—stop. The old man has her—stop. The boxer has her—stop. If he has her in an absurd position—laughter and bravos from the audience. If he has her in a position of exaggerated sophistication, the audience falls silent and analyzes. There's so much merriment and hubbub that it is hard to hear the distant, heavy echoes of artillery on the nearby front. And of course there is no way—not because of *Emmanuelle*, but the great distance—to hear the roaring motors of the armored column moving along the road.

"When the dawn breaks, to Thee, O Lord, the earth sings." A bad sign—Dona Cartagina is singing the Office of Our Lady. Since morning the whole city has been staggering and trembling, and the windowpanes are rattling because the artillery has opened fire all out: boom, boom, bash, whammer-jammer, zoom, zoom, and the horizon is full of martial crashing. Holden Roberto has announced that he will enter Luanda today. He's asked the populace to remain calm. Yesterday his planes dropped leaflets, pictures of Holden with the caption GOD RULES IN HEAVEN HOLDEN RULES ON EARTH.

They must be attacking in great strength, because the firing has not slackened since dawn and it is almost noon. In the city there is panic and nervous running around and shouting. It is fifteen minutes by car to the front line. They may get in. Dona Cartagina wants to hide me in her apartment. She lives near here: Go three blocks and take a right. I'm supposed to go now, and she will show me the way so I'll know. I'll be her son, caring for his elderly, ailing mother. And why do you speak such strange Portuguese? they ask. Because I was born in Timor but I ran away from home and went to live in Burma. I served in the Burmese navy and so I speak that language better.

Show us your documents!

I left my documents on the ship, and you know yourselves that all the ships have sailed away.

Dona Cartagina orders me to burn my papers and pack my suitcase but I tell her no, there's still time, they might not come today.

I call the Cubans; no answer.

I go downstairs, catch Oscar on the run, and ask him what's going on. He doesn't know and he's running. An army truck goes down the street, then another one. Some women with bundles, on the trot. Finally, a patrol appears, looking for the enemy. What enemy? says Felix, as white as the wall. My skin tingles because at that moment I am sitting in front of the telex trying to make contact with Warsaw, but they might think I'm trying to contact Holden Roberto. I have already managed to ring through to the local central and transmit:

```
3322 TIVOLI AN
OB INT LUANDA AN
   ESTIMADO COLLEGA, PODE LIGARME COM POLONIA
NUMERO 814251 OK?
```

But they suddenly disconnect me and I breathe with relief, because one of the patrol has come up to me and wants to see what I have written, but I haven't written anything yet, so he says, We have to be alert, *camarada*, because the enemy is outside Luanda. Yes, *camarada*, I say, and Felix says, Yes, for sure, that's clear, and Oscar, suspended in midstride, also becomes a yes-man, anything to get them to lower their gun barrels or, better yet, leave.

In the end they moved out and I walked through the empty streets to *Diario de Luanda*, to Queiroz, who always knew a lot. Three people produced the newspaper. It had sixteen pages, of which Queiroz wrote eight each day. He thought they were shorthanded: It takes five people to put out a newspaper. He showed me the headlines that had been sent to the printer: "Everyone to the front! The hour of truth has arrived! We won't yield an inch!" He told me that the situation was critical, that all the FNLA forces and five battalions from Zaïre and more mercenaries were attacking, and that the MPLA was sending units from the provinces to the battlefield outside Luanda, but there was no transportation and ammunition was running out.

I went back to the hotel and waited for Warsaw. The reception area was full of people who were afraid to spend the night at home and preferred to sit there and wait for whatever came next. The barrages were coming closer and closer and again there were trucks on the street with no lights.

Suddenly the telex lit up and the machine began:

3322 TIVOLI AN
814251 PAP PL

GOOD EVENING WE CANNOT CONNECT TRY EVERY FEW MINUTES BUT DID NOT MAKE CONTACT AND DO NOT KNOW

WHY MACHINE KEEPS PRINTING BUSY SIGNAL PLEASE

YES BI BI THERE IS A WAR HERE AND TERRIBLE MESS
YESTERDAY SHELL HIT CABLE AND BROKE LINE BUT
FIXED TODAY

BI BI IS DUTY EDITOR THERE?

YES MOM MOM
MORAWSKI HERE

HEY ZDZICH LISTEN STORMING OF LUANDA UNDER WAY
WE MAY LOSE CONTACT HEAVY ARTILLERY BOMBARD-
MENT WILL SEND WHAT I HAVE BUT YOU MUST BE PRE-
PARED FOR LOSS OF CONTACT NOW MATERIAL OK???

YES SIR SEND BUT CANT WE DO SOMETHING RE YOUR
SECURITY PERHAPS CAN ARRANGE AIRPLANE TO GET YOU
OUT

NO TOO LATE EVERYTHING PERHAPS OVER TOMORROW
NOBODY KNOWS WHAT WILL HAPPEN HERE WE ARE VERY
WEAK ITS BAD BUT NOW MATERIAL AND CHAT LATER BE-
CAUSE IM HOMESICK OK?

OK OK SEND

MOM MOM

(I sent "MOM MOM," which means "just a moment,"
because just then the voice of the MPLA chief of staff,
Commandante Xiyetu, came over the radio to announce
a general mobilization. I listened to the end and immediately typed:)

LAST MINUTE LUANDA PAP 2310 IN VIEW OF CRITI-
CAL SITUATION WHICH HAS ARISEN IN ANGOLA GEN-
ERAL STAFF OF MPLA PEOPLES ARMY HAS ANNOUNCED
GENERAL MOBILIZATION OF ALL MEN BETWEEN 18 AND

45 AS OF THURSDAY PM A MOMENT AGO. STAFF COMMU-
NIQUE STATES THAT ANGOLA HAS NOW BECOME VICTIM
OF ARMED AGGRESSION ON WIDE SCALE. ENEMY HAS
CAPTURED A RANGE OF IMPORTANT CITIES TODAY AND
HIS OFFENSIVE IS CONTINUING. FIGHTING NOW UN-
DER WAY IN OUTSKIRTS OF LUANDA. SITUATION IS VERY
SERIOUS AND STAFF COMMUNIQUE ORDERS ALL PA-
TRIOTS TO TAKE UP ARMS AND GO TO FRONT TO DEFEND
COUNTRY END ITEM

MOM MOM

RYSIEK: TELEVISION REQUESTED WE PASS FOLLOW-
ING NOTE TO YOU: ON NOVEMBER 8 WE ARE BROADCAST-
ING PROGRAM ABOUT INTERNAL SITUATION IN ANGOLA
AND WE INVITE YOU TO APPEAR. FILM REPORT WOULD
BE BEST BUT IT COULD ALSO BE DONE WITH STILLS AND
INFORMATION RECORDED ON AUDIO TAPE OR EVEN A
WRITTEN REPORT WHICH WOULD BE READ BY SPECIALLY
HIRED ACTOR. WARMEST REGARDS.

LISTEN RYSIU I SENT THAT NOTE REALIZING HOW
ABSURD IT ALL IS AT THIS MOMENT

DONT WORRY LISTEN TELL CZARNECKI: MICHAL IT
IS GETTING VERY BAD HERE. ASSAULT ON LUANDA COULD
COME ANY DAY WITH LOSS OF COMMUNICATIONS. THAT
IS WHY I WANT TO SET IT UP LIKE THIS: IF YOU CAN-
NOT GET THROUGH TO ME EVENINGS AT AGREED TIME TRY
TO CONNECT MORNING OF NEXT DAY AT 7 GMT AND AGAIN
AT 20 GMT AND AGAIN NEXT DAY UNTIL WE CONNECT AND
GOD GRANTS WE ARE IN TOUCH OK. ARRANGE TO SUS-
PEND ANY POSSIBLE TRAVEL TO LUANDA UNLESS SOME-
BODY IS PLANNING SUICIDE OK? HUGS RYSIEK

YES OK THANKS KEEPING OUR FINGERS CROSSED

THANKS OLD MAN BEST WISHES FROM LUANDA AND IM
WAITING TO HEAR FROM YOU TOMORROW AT 20 GMT OK?

TKS GOODNIGHT

I stood up from the machine drenched in sweat but
glad to have sent such fresh news, straight off the radio.
After midnight I phoned Queiroz. The attack had been
held off, but there were a lot of casualties.

At night I go onto the balcony, point the antenna in the
direction of the bay, and search for distant stations with
my transistor radio. Yes, normal life exists somewhere,
and all you have to do is put your ear to the speaker and
listen. One hemisphere is snoring and tossing from side
to side while the other one is getting up, boiling the
milk, shaving, and powdering. And then the other way
around. A person wakes up and doesn't think that the
last day of his life could be beginning. A splendid feeling, but already so normal that nobody there pays any
attention to it. Hundreds if not thousands of radio stations are working every second and a sea of words is
surging into the air. It's interesting to hear the way the
world argues, agitates, and persuades; how it threat-
ens, how it shams and lies; how everybody is right and
doesn't want to hear the other side. Right now the whole
world is worried about Angola and here Paris, there
London, Cairo, and Tokyo are talking about it. The world
contemplates the great spectacle of combat and death,
which is difficult for it to imagine in the end, because
the image of war is not communicable—not by the pen,
or the voice, or the camera. War is a reality only to those

stuck in its bloody, dreadful, filthy insides. To others it is pages in a book, pictures on a screen, nothing more. I manipulate the transistor, which goes quiet because the batteries are running down (I won't get new ones); I listen to what the distant radio stations are saying. Various voices are scattering ideas and suggestions. What to do with Angola? Call an international conference. Send in United Nations troops and let them separate the brawlers there. But who will pay for that, with the inflation we have? So let an all-black army go and the Arabs can pay for it. The Arabs don't know what to do with money. The best thing would be to call on the Angolans to come to an agreement. Let them sign a ceasefire, let them divvy up the seats of power, let them make it up. Warn them that if they don't make it up, they won't get any more money. Make love, not war. A million-strong Cuban army stands on the border of South Africa. There, in the dry bush, among barefoot tribes fleeing in panic, in that place without roads, without lights, without schools, without cities—there, the fate of contemporary civilization is being decided. Give Vorster help; give him the green light. Endow him with moral support!

Great plans, global strategies.

Overseas they don't know that it all comes down to two people here.

One of them is Ruiz, a congenial and lively Portuguese, the pilot of an old two-engine DC-3, the only plane that the MPLA has in Luanda. The machine was built in 1943; the motors spit gobs of soot, the wings are patched, the tires are bald, the fuselage is full of holes. Only Ruiz knows how to close the door, and it's not easy for him. He flies this plane day and night; he is in the air around the clock. Ruiz flies to Brazzaville for ammunition, and then to a besieged city in the Angolan borderlands to drop off cartridge boxes and bags of flour and take the serious casualties back to Luanda. If Ruiz doesn't arrive on time the cities will have to surrender and the wounded will die. In a sense, the fate of the war rests on his shoulders. Ruiz flies around Angola by memory because there are no air controllers; I don't even know if his plane's radio works. Often he himself doesn't know who holds the airport where he is supposed to land. Yesterday it was still in our hands, but today it could belong to the enemy. That's why he first flies over the airport without landing. Sometimes he recognizes the silhouettes of his acquaintances, so he descends and lands peacefully. Sometimes, however, they start firing on the plane, in which case he turns back and delivers the bad news to Luanda. In this country without transport or communication, Ruiz knows what's happening on the fronts and which cities belong to whom. He takes off at dawn, makes several trips a day, and returns at midnight. Starved soldiers in Luso, the dying garrison in Novo Redondo, and the cut-off defenders of Quibala are waiting for his plane. Now Luanda, which can't hold out without ammunition, is waiting. The best place to find him is at the airport, when he is inspecting the motors early in the morning. Trouble with one of the motors could ground the plane and change the course of the war. There are no spare parts, no mechanics. And the plane is needed constantly. In a moment, Ruiz disappears into the cockpit. The propellers rotate, the plane is lost in thick, impenetrable clouds of black smoke and, thumping, rattling, grinding, the decrepit pile of scrap heaves toward takeoff.

The second person on whom everything depends now

is Alberto Ribeiro, a short, heavyset thirty-year-old engineer. The northern front stretches near Luanda, along the Bengo River. On the banks of this river stands the pumping station that supplies water to Luanda. If the station is out of action, there is no water in the city. The enemy knows this and constantly bombards it. Sometimes they hit the pumps and they stop working. Luanda can take five days without water, no more. In the tropics people can stand the thirst no longer, and epidemics break out besides. The only person who can repair the pumps is Alberto. Thanks to him, the city has water from time to time; it can exist and defend itself. If Alberto were killed in an automobile accident on the way to the station or hit by a shell, Luanda would have to surrender after a few days.

General mobilization. Long lines of young men, mostly unemployed. Instead of holding up a wall, it's better to do your duty—in the army, you get something to eat. They'll soon be fighting and killing. Work at last, even glory. Packed off by their mothers and wives, a lot of women with big bellies. People will give birth and kill until the end of the world. Those who are now seeing the light of day will be twenty-five in the year 2000. Grand celebrations of the dawn of a new millennium. Meetings between youth and the veterans of the twentieth century. An interview with a spry old dame who lived through World War I. An impressive memory and dauntless coquetry to boot, the old lady mentioning how the army was marching through once and up in the hayloft she and a certain soldier, well, yes sir, I've got this straight, I remember it very clearly. Half of humanity will have slant eyes. Half of humanity will not understand what the other half is saying. Time to perfect methods of communicating by signs, time to begin instructions in sign language. The white race will enter the vestigial phase. Barely thirteen percent of the inhabitants of earth will have white skin. Barely two percent will have naturally blond hair. Blondes: a more and more distinctive phenomenon, a rarity of rarities. Which is better—to think or not to think about the future? Future shock: the travails of postindustrial society, luxury. For others, everyday problems: What can we find to eat today? The Bantu language has no future tense; the concept of the future doesn't exist for the Bantu people, they are not tormented by the thought of what will happen in a month, in a year (see the Reverend Father Placide Tempels, *La Philosophie bantoue*). The inductees are led in groups straight to the front. So raw and green—why? To create a false crowd, more confusion? The registration center closes at 6 P.M. People drift away and disappear into the labyrinths of the *musseques*, the poor quarter. The day, quite ordinary, even peaceful, ends.

Meanwhile it turned humid. The guns fell silent at the approaches to Luanda and there was no news from the other fronts. It seemed that time had stopped, that nothing was happening. The sails of our ship went slack and we found ourselves becalmed. Waiting for the storm. I felt that there was nothing to breathe. This was a special kind of oppressiveness, not to be measured in millibars. You felt it psychologically rather than physically. An invisible vise was tightening, intensifying the sense of danger and fear. I thought that it might be my own private condition, my individual depression. I started observing others. They all had the faces of people who find it oppressive. Dull, expressionless faces with smudged expressions, lacking strength, lacking charm. The feeling of closeness was so acute that all you had to do was start talking on any random topic, and soon you would be hearing that it was stifling. People had trouble talking about anything else. At all events these were unclear, foggy disclosures, because the feeling of oppressiveness is a very difficult state to define. Usually you only say that something is hanging in the air, something has to happen, something is awaiting us. There being a war on, your interlocutor states that blood will flow. This is a lesson drawn from history, and history teaches that crucial events cannot occur without bloodshed. Then comes the moment of silence in which you wonder whether it's going to be *your* blood. A state of irritation and restlessness accompanies the feeling of closeness. A person unable to grasp the situation and eager to enlighten himself pays heed to the most fantastic rumors. He is afraid, he acts out irrational impulses, the herd instinct in him is easily aroused.

It becomes oppressive when important events, important changes, can't break through to the surface of life and are continually unable to fulfill themselves. The still invisible and uncrystallized fact that is to be realized in the future is already growing, swelling, beginning to push through into a preexisting reality which, however, doesn't want to yield. It gets tighter and tighter, and therefore more and more suffocating. The lack of air increases our feeling of helplessness. We watch the gathering of the clouds and wait for a voice to speak from them, reading us the inexorable verdict of fate.

GOOD EVENING [Warsaw comes through] COPY PLEASE

UNFORTUNATELY, I STILL HAVE NO INFORMATION.
APPARENT CALM PREVAILS AND NOTHING IS HAPPEN-
ING, TYPICAL CALM BEFORE THE STORM. WE KNOW THAT
THE INVASION IS CONTINUING BUT THERE IS NO NEWS
FROM THE FRONT, BAD DAYS ARE COMING BUT THAT IS
NOT CONCRETE INFORMATION FOR PRINT. CALL TO-
MORROW, MAYBE SOMETHING WILL HAPPEN

OK, TILL TOMORROW THEN

TILL TILL TKS

TKS BYE

BYE

Somebody pounded on my door at two in the morning. I snapped out of a deep sleep, and the flesh stood
up on the back of my neck because I thought: FNLA!

I trudged on leaden legs to open the door. Three incredibly filthy types tumbled into the room. They threw
themselves on me and I threw myself on them and we
started hugging and shouting—it was Nelson, Manuel,
and Bota! They laid their weapons on the floor and
wanted to wash. Then Nelson dived onto the bed and
fell asleep in a second, while the others started opening
the one can of meat that I'd been saving for my hour of
need.

What's going on at the southern front? I asked.

There is no southern front, Manuel said; they're already outside Benguela. The second column is headed
for Luanda.

Can't they be stopped?

That's a tough one. They command enormous firepower. They have a lot of armor, a lot of artillery, they fight well, and they're determined. We have nothing to fight with. Our men aren't prepared to stand up to a regular army. We're withdrawing because the forces are unequal.

What about Farrusco?

We don't know; he was badly wounded.

Did you see them close up?

Yes. They have Panhard armored personnel carriers, very fast. They're mobile and they know the terrain well. They split up into groups of five or six vehicles and keep changing positions. They're everywhere and nowhere, and it's hard to catch them. We don't have the resources to organize a defense.

When will they get to Luanda?

In a few days, perhaps.

The pessimistic side of my nature suggested that the moment of annihilation had come and the end was approaching. All they would have to do was take the power plant at Cambamba, close to two hundred kilometers from Luanda. Electricity runs from there to the pumping station; whether the city has water or not depends on that power plant. Without water and light, the surrounded and starved city would have to lay down its arms after a few days.

Monday, November 3 (Judgment Day)

Morning—nothing.

Noon—Pablo comes for me in the jeep at the assigned point. There are two more Cubans with him. They are wearing green fatigues with no insignia. The only distinguishing mark is the weapons on their shoulders.

Nobody asks an armed man what he is doing. As soon as he says "*Cubano*," the patrols run out of questions and he can drive on. We pass an industrial park thrown up in the fields. Then the pastures—regular, well-maintained rectangles of succulent grass—begin. Herds of stray cows: tons of meat and milk, with nobody watching them. There is hunger in the city, but nobody bothers the cattle—this is Portuguese property, untouchable. A short way down the road, gentle hills begin, heaps of earth, lines of entrenchments, artillery, tents, crates—the northern front, the soft underbelly of the war because these are the approaches to Luanda. The view from the first line of trenches: the countryside spread out green, a river in a shallow valley, an asphalt road, a blown bridge, the shot-up pumping station, a palm grove. On the other side, in the distance, a sunlit hill, the enemy's fortifications. Through the lenses of powerful binoculars I can see specks of dust and horizontal and vertical scales; figures are running back and forth, and vehicles are moving along the horizontal scale: preparations for an attack. On the side where we are, there is also a great deal of movement, sandbags are being passed about, outposts camouflaged, artillery shunted. They don't want to be taken by surprise. Then come night, dawn, and waiting—who will strike first? Someone finally does strike, the other side replies, dust rises from the earth, the dance of fire and death begins. Pablo walks around giving orders and checking supplies like a boy with candles on Christmas Eve. I walk behind him, taking pictures. They all want to be photographed. Me now, me now, *camarada*, me, meeeeeeeeee! They stand rigidly and some of them salute. To leave a trace, to fix themselves, to remain somehow. I was here, just yesterday I was here, he took a picture, yes, that's how I looked. That's the kind of face I had as a live man. I stand before you at attention: Look at me for a moment before you turn to something else.

Afternoon—we were on our way back to the city, when the jeep drove down a side street and stopped in front of a one-story villa where the Cuban advisers had their headquarters. We had barely managed to sit down when a soldier ran in and handed Pablo a sheet of paper torn out of a notebook with a message written on it in pencil.

Pablo read it and went pale.

Without a word, he went out onto the veranda and sat down on a bench. He took out a handkerchief and began wiping his forehead. We waited for him to say something. He read the message again and remained silent, until at last he said quietly, indistinctly, as if his mouth were stiff:

"They captured Benguela today. All the Cubans died in the fighting for the town. Word was sent by a wounded signalman."

Then he looked at us and added:

"Now they're on their way to Luanda. It's six hundred kilometers from Benguela to Luanda, but there are no strongpoints or defensive lines along the way. If those are gutsy boys and they decide to drive night and day, they can be here tomorrow."

In the next house a woman called out "Mauro! Mauro!" After a moment, a child's voice answered. It was 6 P.M. The Angelus sounded somewhere far off.

"Get me the radio operator," Pablo said to the soldier who had brought the message. "And dismiss the men."

Military matters were beginning, so I withdrew and went to the hotel. I asked someone to drive me to the edge of the city, to Moro da Luz, where the MPLA headquarters was located in the former residence of the French consul. But the staff was meeting and the sentry didn't want to admit me. I went back in a truck carrying Portuguese soldiers. These were troops in a state of utter dissoluteness. They wore long beards and had neither caps nor belts. They were selling their rations on the black market and breaking into cars. Their orders were to maintain neutrality, not to shoot, not to get involved. They were loading everything onto the ships. The last unit was to leave in a week.

In the evening I spoke with Queiroz. He thinks Luanda will be hard for them to take, because the whole populace will fight and they will have to decide on a mass slaughter that the world might not tolerate. But then he began to have doubts himself: "In the end, how can I know? The world is so far away."

Ruiz flies the plane to Porto Amboim, carrying a group of sappers and some crates of dynamite. They are to blow all the bridges on the Cuvo River, which will cut the road between Benguela and Luanda. If they make it.

Warsaw calls at midnight.

THE SITUATION IN ANGOLA [I sent] HAS TAKEN A DRAMATIC TURN IN THE LAST TWENTY-FOUR HOURS. THE SOUTH AFRICAN ARMY, SUPPORTED BY UNITS OF MERCENARIES AND THE FNLA AND UNITA, HAS OCCUPIED BENGUELA, THE SECOND LARGEST CITY IN ANGOLA. THESE TROOPS ARE PROCEEDING IN TWO STRONG ARMORED COLUMNS TOWARD THE CAPITAL, WHERE THE DEFENSE OF THE CITY IS BEING ORGANIZED. ACCORDING TO STILL UNCONFIRMED REPORTS JUST RECEIVED

HERE, ONE OF THESE COLUMNS HAS OCCUPIED NOVO
REDONDO AND IS THREE HUNDRED MILES SOUTH OF
LUANDA. IF THESE TROOPS CANNOT BE STOPPED AT THE
LINE OF THE CUVO RIVER THEY COULD BE AT THE AP-
PROACHES TO LUANDA WITHIN THE NEXT TWO DAYS. IT
IS ANTICIPATED THAT A SIMULTANEOUS ATTACK WOULD
THEN BEGIN FROM THE NORTH AND THE SOUTH IN AC-
CORDANCE WITH PLAN ORANGE, WHICH CALLS FOR THE
OCCUPATION OF THE CAPITAL BEFORE NOVEMBER 10.
THIS WOULD MEAN THE POLITICAL AND MILITARY LIQ-
UIDATION OF THE MPLA, AT LEAST IN THE SHORT TERM
END ITEM.

FRIENDS, CALL ME IN SEVEN HOURS BECAUSE THIS
IS THE DECISIVE MOMENT, OK?

YES, OF COURSE, TKS MUCH

TKS BYE BYE

GOOD NIGHT

Tuesday, November 4 (nerves, nerves)

I got up at three in the morning, to prepare my com-
mentary for PAP in peace. I had barely gone downstairs
and got the telex working, however, when in walked
five toughs with automatics, heading straight for me:
"Sit down and don't move!" They woke up Felix, who
was sleeping like a rock on the couch, and demanded a
list of the hotel guests. They were going to conduct a
search and take everybody to the police for interrogation. The enemy is inside the city, in this quarter, in this
hotel. Fifth column. Infiltration. They brought a dozen
or more sleepy, frightened people downstairs. Persua-

118

sion was senseless. "No talking!" cried the leader, holding up his pistol like the starter at a track meet. You ought to go blow off some steam on the front, brother, I wanted to tell him. We waited some more, but organization had broken down as usual, and the car that was supposed to take us to the police had not showed up. Almeyda, the MPLA press chief, appeared with the morning. He ordered them to let us go and told them to leave. People walked away dejected and exhausted. Anybody with a pistol could go around terrorizing hotels, doing whatever he wanted.

Quiet reigns on the northern front. They are waiting for the troops from the south to come nearer. Then they will strike from two sides at once—this week, perhaps tomorrow.

Radio communiqués summon the populace to the defense of the city. In this decisive hour. No one can shirk.

The MPLA leadership meets all day.

Help is apparently waiting in Brazzaville and in Kabinda, but it can't reach Luanda because the airport and the harbor remain in the hands of the Portuguese army until next Monday (November 10). Until next Monday, Angola is formally a Portuguese territory, an overseas province, and also a part of NATO territory. So the MPLA must hold out until next week. And if it is too late? If the Portuguese units suddenly strike Luanda itself, attacking the Angolans? (There are fears that some units, led by rightist officers, will abandon neutrality and begin operating on their own.) Rumors circulate that President Neto has already been arrested. Panic breaks out. It is impossible to get a grip on the situation. A complete lack of information from the southern front. Where is the enemy? Have they halted? Are they coming? Still far away? Already in the suburbs? People are losing their heads. I drop by my room and find that Dona Cartagina has packed my bag herself. And where are the newspaper clippings that I have been collecting for three months, my greatest treasure? Where are the clippings? She threw them into the toilet and flushed them! (It was my misfortune that Ribeiro had fixed the pumps that day and there was water.)

Reports spread that the MPLA will announce independence ahead of time—today or tomorrow—counting on immediate recognition of Angola by friendly countries who will treat the airport and harbor as sovereign territory of the new state. Access to Luanda is the issue. Right now, the decisive thing is to open the city, which is surrounded on land and cannot be reached by water or air.

And if help doesn't come in time? The storming of Luanda. Despite the heroic efforts of the city's inhabitants, the overwhelming strength of the enemy, etc. Who will come in first? The ones from the south or the FNLA? The FNLA is a cruel army. They practice cannibalism. A few days ago I didn't believe that. But last week I went with a group of local journalists to Lucala, four hundred kilometers east of Luanda. One day earlier, Lucala had been recaptured from an FNLA unit that withdrew to Samba Caju, a town seventy kilometers to the north. We drove with a pursuing unit. The seventy kilometers were a horrible sight. All along the road through this thickly populated region, there was not a single living person or surviving house. All the people had been murdered and all the villages burned. The withdrawing army had destroyed every sign of life along the way. Heads of women had been thrown in the roadside grass. Corpses with hearts and livers cut out. I rode half the way with my eyes closed. At one point, somebody in our car raised his voice. I opened my eyes: In a dead, burned village two monkeys were sitting at a table in front of a burned bar. They looked at us for a moment and then made tracks for the bushes.

To fall into the hands of drunken cannibals—a grim death. Their sweaty faces, their dull gaze, the way they shout, the way they point their guns at their victims, their amusement at the trembling they inspire in them. Better not to think about it.

In the evening Commandante Ju-Ju reads his daily radio communiqué on the situation at the front. Very optimistic. Upsetting, that. Reality looks bad; half the country is in enemy hands, yet from what Ju-Ju reads, the MPLA seem to be on the brink of victory.

Don't take reality into account

—A principle which is intended to function like a sleeping pill. Don't panic, don't lapse into doubt, don't get hysterical. But how can you talk people into acting now, at the decisive moment, without making them aware of the full gravity of the situation? They won't move; they'll lie there and chew the cud of optimism. Since things are so good, why exert yourself? And these disorienting contradictions: Here an appeal to defend the city, and there it appears that everything is as good as can be. The result: a loss of faith. In the hour of decision, they are not going to trust anyone; even their instinct of self-preservation is being blunted.

3322 TIVOLI AN
814251 PAP PL
   GOOD EVENING PLS MATERIAL

SORRY I DIDNT SEND ANYTHING MORNING AND DIDNT EVEN CALL BUT THE POLICE LOCKED US UP FOR NO REASON. PEOPLE SIMPLY LOSING HEADS. NO WONDER WHEN THEY THINK THEY MIGHT DIE SOON. CALL ME IN MORNING AT 7 GMT THERE COULD BE SENSATIONAL NEWS AND MAYBE THIS TIME THEY WONT SHUT ME DOWN OK???

YES UNTIL 7 GMT IN MORNING OK

OK BI BI WAITING ANXIOUSLY

VIA ITT 11.4.75 1407 EDT

Queiroz called during the night and said that the Portuguese army would leave the civilian part of the airport and withdraw from the harbor tomorrow. If true, this is really sensational news. A glimmer of salvation. God, what a relief! I jumped to the ceiling with joy.

Wednesday, November 5 (landing)

This evening I went to the airport with Oscar's friend Gilberto, who works in the control tower. Dark, a horrible downpour: we drove as if under a fountain, no visibility, only walls of water through which our Peugeot burrowed and I felt as if I were in a subway moving through the streets of a submerged city. The large glass airport terminal building—monstrously littered and dirty because no one had cleaned up after the half million refugees who had camped here—was empty. I stood on the second floor with Gilberto, looking at the illuminated runway. The tropical deluge had passed, but it was still raining. High up to the left, two spotlights suddenly appeared: A plane was coming in to land. A moment later, it touched down and taxied between two rows of yellow lights. A Cubana Airlines Britannia. Then more and more spotlights up above. Four planes landed. They maneuvered into a row in front of us, the pilots switched off the engines, and it was quiet. The stairs were wheeled into place and Cuban soldiers with packs and weapons began disembarking. They lined up in two rows. They were wearing camouflage, which afforded some protection from the rain. After a few minutes, they walked toward trucks waiting nearby. My shoulder felt sore. I smiled: Through the whole scene, Gilberto had been gripping my shoulder tightly.

Those soldiers went to the front the next day.

The hotel grew crowded and noisy. Neto was supposed to proclaim the independence of Angola late Monday night, and an aircraft had brought umpteen foreign correspondents from Lisbon for the occasion. They were given visas and lodged in our hotel. Oscar was tearing his hair in desperation because there was nothing to give them to eat, but they cheered him up by saying that food wasn't important. Information was important.

What stories the world press publishes! I read many of the dispatches sent from Luanda in those days. I admired the opulence of human fantasy. But I also understood my colleagues' predicament. The editor sends a reporter to a country that is fascinating to the entire world. Such a journey costs a lot of money. The world is waiting for a great story, a scoop, a sensational narrative written under a hail of bullets. The special correspondent flies out to Luanda. He is taken to the hotel. He gets a room, shaves, and changes his shirt. He is ready and goes out immediately to look for the fighting.

After several hours he announces that he's beating his head against a wall—

He can't do anything.

Angola betrays no interest in his presence. The telephone doesn't answer, or if it does it answers in Portuguese, a language he doesn't understand. If he has enough strength and endurance, he can make the journey on foot to Government Palace. There he meets Elvira, a moon-faced typist who will smile but knows nothing and isn't telling what she does know. He might meet young Costa, who will answer all questions by shaking his head and remaining silent. Make the trip to MPLA headquarters? That's an all-day journey, and besides, the guard won't let him through the gate. Go to President Neto! But how? Nobody will say where the President lives. Ride to the front. To what front? You can't travel outside Luanda; it's a closed city. A group of Frenchmen acquired a car somewhere and decided, without looking into anything, to drive to the northern front. They were stopped at the first checkpoint and delivered straight to the airport. See a Cuban! But how? They are nowhere to be seen. Is Luso in MPLA hands? Because Savimbi says that UNITA holds it. Who knows? There has been no contact with that city for a long time. It's essential to find out exactly where the front is. Where the front is? Who could know that? Even at headquarters, nobody is sure.

There are some remaining sources of information: Dona Cartagina, Oscar, and Felix. Dona Cartagina is now busy cleaning and has no time for politics. In any case, she speaks only Portuguese and it's hard to communicate with her. Oscar invariably repeats MPLA slogans: *A victoria e certa!* Victory is certain. But that is skimpy and, moreover, not exactly what everyone is looking for. Felix gives the most matter-of-fact and truthful answers. Asked about the situation, he answers tersely: *Confusão*.

Confusão is a good word, a synthesis word, an everything word. In Angola it has its own specific sense and is literally untranslatable. To simplify things: *Confusão* means confusion, a mess, a state of anarchy and disorder. *Confusão* is a situation created by people, but in the course of creating it they lose control and direction, becoming victims of *confusão* themselves. There is a sort of fatalism in *confusão*. A person wants to do something, but it all falls to pieces in his hands; he wants to set something in motion, but some power paralyzes him; he wants to create something, but he produces *confusão*. Everything crosses him; even with the best will in the world, he falls over and over again into *confusão*. *Confusão* can overwhelm our thinking, and then others will say that the person has *confusão* in his head. It can steal into our hearts, and then our girls dump us. It can explode in a crowd and sweep through a mass of people— then there is fighting, death, arson. Sometimes *confusão* takes a more benign form in which it assumes the character of desultory, chaotic, but bloodless haggling.

Confusão is a state of absolute disorientation. People who have found themselves on the inside of *confusão* can't comprehend what is going on around them or in themselves. Nor can they explain specifically what caused this particular case of *confusão*. There are carriers who spread *confusão*, and others must beware, though this is difficult because literally any person can at any moment become a perpetrator of *confusão*, even against his will. By *confusão* we also understand our own states of perplexity and helplessness. We see *confusão* raging around

125

us and can't do anything to stop it. *Camaradas*, we hear again and again, don't make *confusão*—don't! But does it depend on us? The most precise report from the front: What's new with you? *Confusão!* Everyone who understands this word knows the whole story. *Confusão* can reign over an enormous territory and sweep through millions of people. Then there is a war. A state of *confusão* can't be broken at one stroke or liquidated in the blinking of an eye. Anyone who tries falls into *confusão* himself. The best thing is to act slowly and wait. After a while *confusão* loses energy, weakens, vanishes. We emerge from a state of *confusão* exhausted, but somehow satisfied that we have managed to survive. We start gathering strength again for the next *confusão*.

How to explain all this to people who have been in Luanda only a few hours? So once again, as if they hadn't heard him, they ask Felix:

"What's the situation?"

And Felix answers:

"Haven't I told you already? *Confusão*."

They go away shaking their heads and shrugging their shoulders. And they are shaking their heads and shrugging their shoulders because Felix has sown *confusão* among them.

The next four days were drowned in unusual *confusão*. Every so often someone came into the hotel shouting, "They're coming! They're coming!" and announced breathlessly that the armored vehicles of the Afrikaners were already at the city's edge. According to one, they were painted yellow; according to another, green. Numerous figures were given: Ten of these vehicles had been seen, later fifty or more. There was no way to check: They might really be a few kilometers away, or those might have been mere rumors. Oscar hung a map of Angola behind the reception desk. A crowd of people stood before it, arguing. Everyone wanted to show with his finger where in his opinion the front was, who had what city, to whom this or that road belonged. No two of them had the same picture of the situation. After a few days, the hundreds of fingers sweeping across the map had rubbed out cities, roads, and rivers. The country looked like a fragment of a gray, naked planet without people or nature.

On Monday the Portuguese garrison sailed away. The last platoon climbed the gangplank to the ship that morning. I knew some of the officers there and I went to say good-bye to them. The locals wanted the garrison to leave as quickly as possible. After years of colonial war, there could be neither understanding nor friendship between the two sides. But I saw it differently. I knew that in this final period the Angolans owed a large debt of gratitude to many, though not all, of the Portuguese officers. They had known how to behave loyally. I myself owed them a lot. They had treated me with sympathy and helped me generously. Nor had they ever attacked the Cubans, although the first people from Havana had come here when Angola was still formally a part of Portuguese territory. There exists a kind of interpersonal solidarity that should not be destroyed by dry political calculation.

A truck drove around the city that day and removed the statues of the Portuguese conquerors from their pediments. The governors and the generals, the travelers and the explorers were collected in front of the citadel and arranged in two brown granite rows. The plazas and squares looked even emptier. That afternoon an airplane flew in carrying foreign delegations. Only a few came. Rumors were circulating around the world that a squadron from Zaïre would bomb the airport that day and there would be no return. The cautious majority waited in their own countries for the unfolding of events in our city. It seems that they were right, because—as emerged later—the decision to destroy the airport had been reversed only at the last minute.

Thousands of people gathered at night in one of the squares. There had been requests to avoid large crowds so as to prevent a massacre in case of attack. The night was dark and cloudy, and the scene at the assembly recalled the secret meetings of the Kimbangists.

The cathedral clock struck twelve.

November 11, 1975.

Quiet reigned on the square. From the speakers' platform, Agostinho Neto read a text proclaiming the People's Republic of Angola. His voice broke and he had to pause several times. When he finished, there was applause from the invisible crowd, and the people cheered. There were no more speeches. After a moment the lights on the platform went out and everyone departed rather hastily, lost in the darkness. On the northern front the artillery was silent. But suddenly the soldiers in town began shooting wildly into the air in celebration. There was a chaotic uproar and the night came alive.

In the Tivoli, Oscar went to the safe and took out a bottle of champagne and a bottle of whisky that he had saved for the occasion. We were the oldest residents of the hotel, a crowd of veterans. Instead of evoking cheer and joy, the alcohol intensified our tiredness, our exhaustion. Oscar, who had long been at the limits of his strength, now drunk, called out in despair, "If this is what independence is like, I'll blow my brains out!" After a moment it dawned on him that this was out of place, so he laughed and then grew quiet; in the end, he fell asleep with his head on the table amid the empty glasses.

There was a reception for the foreign delegations at Government Palace in the morning. I sent a dispatch to Warsaw that day:

LUANDA PAP 11.11. THE INDEPENDENCE CELEBRA-
TIONS TAKING PLACE IN LUANDA HAVE BEEN PEACEFUL
SO FAR. THE HOLIDAY ATMOSPHERE HAS BEEN SPOILED
BY FNLA GUNNERS WHO HAVE AGAIN SHELLED THE
PUMPING STATION AT QUINPANDONGO AND LEFT LUANDA
WITHOUT WATER FOR TWO DAYS. IN THIS CONNECTION,
A WILD STRUGGLE TOOK PLACE TODAY FOR INVITA-
TIONS TO THE RECEPTION THAT PRESIDENT NETO GAVE
AT GOVERNMENT PALACE BECAUSE OF RUMORS THAT IT
WOULD BE POSSIBLE TO DRINK WATER THERE.

A RADIO STATION--NON-ANGOLAN--HAS REPORTED
THAT THE FNLA AND UNITA HAVE DECIDED TO FORM
THEIR OWN GOVERNMENT WITH A CAPITAL IN HUAMBO.
THIS WILL BE ONLY A PRO FORMA CAPITAL SINCE THE
ACTUAL HEADQUARTERS OF THESE ORGANIZATIONS IS
KINSHASA. THUS ANGOLA HAS BEEN DIVIDED FOR THE
MOMENT INTO TWO STATES WITH INCREDIBLY COMPLI-
CATED BORDERS THAT CHANGE ALMOST EVERY DAY
ACCORDING TO WHICH SIDE LAUNCHES AN OFFENSIVE
TODAY OR TOMORROW AND WHAT PART OF THE TERRITORY
IS TAKEN FROM THE ENEMY. NOW MUCH WILL DEPEND ON

WHICH COUNTRIES RECOGNIZE THE MPLA GOVERNMENT
OR THE FNLA—UNITA GOVERNMENT, AND AT WHAT TEMPO.
SO A NEW, DIPLOMATIC WAR FOR ANGOLA HAS BEGUN.

IN THE MEANTIME, THE REAL WAR IS INTENSIFY-
ING. BOTH SIDES ARE GETTING STRONGER. THERE ARE
MORE AND MORE MEN, BETTER—TRAINED TROOPS, AND
WEAPONS OF GREATER DESTRUCTIVE POWER.

ON MONDAY, NOVEMBER 10, THE ENEMY BEGAN A NEW
TWO—FRONT OFFENSIVE. THERE WAS AN ATTEMPT TO
CAPTURE LUANDA FROM THE NORTH. ARMORED VEHI-
CLES AND ARTILLERY TOOK PART IN THE ASSAULT ALONG
WITH COMPANIES OF ZAIRIAN TROOPS AND PORTU-
GUESE MERCENARIES. THE SOUTH AFRICAN ARMY,
WHICH IS MOVING FROM THE SOUTH IN TWO MOBILE AND
POWERFUL ARMORED COLUMNS, IS HEADING FOR PORTO
AMBOIM AND, FURTHER ON, LUANDA. MPLA UNITS IN
THIS AREA ARE ORGANIZING A DEFENSIVE LINE WITH
THE MISSION OF HOLDING PORTO AMBOIM AT ALL COSTS
FIN. COULD YOU SEND A LITTLE MONEY AND SOME CIG-
ARETTES???? TKS IN ADVANCE BYE

Ruiz throttled back: The plane descended toward earth.
We had passed Porto Amboim, a small fishing port, and
flown over the wide, dark Cuvo River; then the plane
flew straight for a few more minutes until it banked and
we started back. Ruiz motioned for me to look through
the windshield. Below, I could see a road that led to the
river and seemed to have dropped into the water, because the bridge across the river had been destroyed.
Now we flew along a road on which I could see a motionless column of armored vehicles. I counted: There
were twenty-one of them and farther on stood trucks

pulling artillery and, at the rear, five jeeps. People wandered along both sides of the road. We returned over the far bank of the river, passing zigzags of trenches below and some units on the road. The plane descended to treetop level and landed on the runway at Porto Amboim airport.

Ruiz had been carrying ammunition and flew straight back to Luanda, but I stayed behind. It was less than twelve miles along the riverbank to the front. A soldier with very dark skin took me there in a car. I asked him in Portuguese if he was from Luanda. No, he answered in Spanish, from Havana. It was hard to tell them apart by sight in those days, because the Cubans had clothed many MPLA units in uniforms they had brought over. This also had a psychological significance, because the FNLA and UNITA troops feared the Cubans most of all. They turned and ran at the sight of units in Cuban uniforms attacking, even though there might not have been a single Cuban among them. External differences were further effaced by the fact that both MPLA and Cuban units were multiracial, so skin color told nothing. Later, this all reinforced the legend of an army of a hundred thousand Cubans fighting in Angola. In truth, the whole army defending the republic came to not more than thirty thousand soldiers, of whom about two-thirds were Angolans.

We drove to a place where there were big cotton warehouses. Front headquarters was located here. You walked around in cotton up to your knees like snow. White moss grew on the uniforms and heads of the soldiers. You slept warm and comfortable here. The front line ran along the river. The South African units couldn't break through because all the bridges had been blown.

They hadn't been prepared for that and were waiting for pontoon bridges. Both sides exchanged sporadic fire but felt too weak to attack. A ship was supposed to arrive the next day with two companies of Cubans and a company from Guinea-Bissau. Two MPLA units were on their way overland.

At dawn we drove along the front. It was pouring rain and piercingly cold. The car skidded in the mud and we had to flounder around on foot. We passed a dispersed unit, a dozen or more soldiers straggling along the road. Each of them was leading a small, barefoot, shivering child by the hand. At night, a few women with children had crossed to this side of the river in primitive African dugouts. The women had stayed at the shore to guard their belongings while the soldiers led the children to the rear, to the kitchen, to feed them.

I returned that same day in Ruiz's airplane. Several badly wounded soldiers, local and Cuban, lay on the floor. There had been a night battle sixty miles east of Porto Amboim when the South Africans tried to force the river. The wounded made no noise; two of them were unconscious. Some African women sat motionless in the corner. The plane flew through clouds, lurching; rain fell below. We landed at Luanda in a downpour. Two heavy Antonovs stood on a side apron. They had brought mortars.

That evening, to Warsaw:

I RETURNED TODAY FROM THE SOUTHERN FRONT, THE BORDER OF WHICH NOW RUNS ALONG THE CUVO RIVER. I WILL LEAVE THE DETAILED DESCRIPTION FOR LATER:

NOW I WANT TO SEND THE BIG NEWS. THE WAR IN ANGOLA HAS CHANGED IN CHARACTER. UNTIL RECENTLY IT WAS PRIMARILY A GUERRILLA WAR, DOMESTIC, FOUGHT WITH LIGHT WEAPONS. THE INTERVENTION OF THE SOUTH AFRICAN ARMY HAS CHANGED THAT. TODAY THIS IS MORE AND MORE A WAR OF REGULAR ARMIES AND HEAVY EQUIPMENT. THE YOUNG REPUBLIC REMAINS IN A DIF-FICULT MILITARY PREDICAMENT, BUT IT HAS A CHANCE TO DEFEND ITSELF. THE ANGOLAN ARMY LEADERSHIP IS CONSOLIDATING ITS FORCES TO GO ON THE OFFEN-SIVE.

SOMETHING ELSE FOR THE FOREIGN DESK.

MICHAL, RYSIEK HERE, LOOK, MY MONEY RAN OUT LONG AGO AND I AM BARELY ALIVE. IT IS MORE OR LESS CLEAR WHAT WILL HAPPEN, WHICH IS THAT THE ANGO-LANS WILL WIN, BUT IT IS GOING TO TAKE A WHILE AND I AM ON MY LAST LEGS. SO I ASK YOU TO GIVE ME PER-MISSION TO RETURN HOME. A PLANE IS SUPPOSED TO LEAVE FOR LISBON, AND IT COULD TAKE ME OK???

YES, AFFIRMATIVE, IF YOU HAVE HAD ENOUGH YOU CAN COME HOME

GREAT, I'LL START ARRANGING DEPARTURE

OK, STRIKE YOUR SAILS, MIREK WILL BE WAITING FOR YOU IN LISBON

Packing and saying good-bye.

Pablo gave me a box of cigars for the road.

Commandante Ju-Ju gave me Davidson's book on Angola.

And Dona Cartagina? Dona Cartagina broke down crying. We have lived through the worst together, and now my eyes were wet, too, when I looked at her. Dona

133

Cartagina, I said, I'll be back. But I didn't know if what I was saying was true.

I also drove over to say good-bye to President Neto. The President lived in a villa outside town, built on a slope above a small, palm-grown cove. We talked about poetry—I was carrying his latest book of verse, *Sagrada Esperança*, which had appeared in Lisbon that year.

> As nossas terras
> vermalhas do café
> brancas de algodão
> verdes dos milharaes
> havemos de voltar
>
> [Our lands
> red as coffee berries
> white as cotton
> green as fields of grain
> we will return]

I knew that by heart. Neto complained that he'd had no time to write poetry lately and nodded toward a wall map, toward the little green and yellow flags stuck in it to indicate the positions of the FNLA and UNITA. A wall of books in his cramped office forms a better background for this figure than a public rostrum (though he is an excellent speaker). I have never seen him in uniform and can't remember him going to the front.

I knew that things were going badly, I wanted to learn the details from him, but at the same time I didn't feel up to asking him questions that would hurt. So there was silence and then I said good-bye and left.

In the evening I brush off my mildewed suit and put on a tie: I'm returning to Europe.

March 27, 1976

The last South African army units withdraw from Angolan territory. They return along the same road that I once drove with Diogenes, and later with Farrusco, eaten by a fear that I will never forget. Where is Farrusco now? Alive, probably. People in Lubango hid him during the invasion, he lay there for a long time, and his wounds finally healed. He was a tough man. I don't know what happened to Diogenes. I would like to think that he's alive, too. Antonio was killed. Carlos was killed. It is calm on all fronts.

Those British mercenaries who escaped from the northern front are already in London, telling what they did in Angola. "Some people," one of them says in a BBC report, "think that war is a nice, light flesh wound in the leg. They're wrong. War is a head smashed to pulp, legs blown off, guys crawling in a circle with their guts spilling out, a guy soaked in napalm but still alive. It hardens you. For instance, you find a wounded Cuban and turn him over on his back, he makes some sort of movement. You think he's going for a gun so you shoot him dead. But maybe he only wanted to pull out a photograph of his wife and say, 'Help me.' And you shot him. You just didn't want to take the risk. If a person fires into a moving wall of people he doesn't look at their faces, doesn't look at the people. He simply shoots at the silhouettes and doesn't connect them with any human beings. When you come up directly on somebody and fight hand to hand, then you see plainly that it's a person just like you, but then your life is usually at stake. You have to kill him before he kills you. I killed my first man when I was seventeen, seventeen and a half, maybe eighteen, in Aden. Later, I had night-mares—battle shock—and I woke up screaming, but now, now I can't even remember what that guy looked like."

Pieter Botha, the defense minister of the Republic of South Africa, passes his army in review as it returns from war across the border bridge over the Cunene River. Although the soldiers cross the bridge in silence, there is a lot of shouting and screaming in the vicinity, since at the same time the FNLA and UNITA units that until that moment had accompanied the white South African soldiers are throwing themselves into the river en masse and splashing across toward Namibia. Many drown in crossing. But the war has ended, the democracy of the front has ended, and the law of segregation applies again: Passage across the bridge is for whites only.